DISCOVERING
ELIZABETHAN LONDON

DISCOVERING ELIZABETHAN LONDON

Diary and Sketches by Arline K. Thomson

 UNIVERSITY OF MAINE PRESS ORONO, MAINE

Library of Congress Card Catalog Number: 94-061950

ISBN: 0-89101-085-8 (Cloth edition)
       0-89101-086-6 (Paper edition)
       0-89101-084-X (Limited, boxed edition)

Manufactured in the United States of America.

First edition.

9 8 7 6 5 4 3 2 1

To my husband, Robert B. Thomson, who first planted the idea for this book and helped in its nurturing, but was unable to see its completion.

Contents

Introduction ix

1   Portesoken Warde 1

2   Tower Streete Warde 8

3   Aldgate Warde 17

4   Limestreete Warde 27

5   Bishopsgate Warde 30

6   Brodestreete Warde 36

7   Cornehill Warde 42

8   Langborne Warde 50

9   Billinsgate Warde 56

10 Bridge Warde Within 62

11 Candlewicke Street Warde 70

12 Walbrooke Warde 74

13 Downegate Warde 80

14 Vintry Warde 84

15 Cordwainer Street Ward 88

16 Cheape Warde 92

17 Coleman Street Warde 102

18 Bassings Hall Warde 107

19 Creplesgate Warde 110

20 Aldersgate Warde 118

21 Faringdon Ward Within 126

22 Bredstreete Warde 140

23 Queene Hithe Warde 142

24 Castle Baynard Warde 147

25 Faringdon Warde Without 152

26 Borough of Southwarke and Bridge Warde Without . . 178

27 The Suburbes Without the Walles 188

28 Liberties of the Dutchie of Lancaster 206

29 The Citie of Westminster 212

Postscript 224

Acknowledgments 227

Appendix 228

A List of Places and Directions
for the Nearest Underground Station 229

A List of Maps 233

Introduction.

"What London hath beene of auncient time, men may here see, as what it is now euery man doth beholde."

A citizen of London, John Stow wrote these words during the reign of the first Queen Elizabeth. I can't think of a better way to introduce this diary and sketches of present day London.

On a January day in 1974 my husband took me for my first walk in London. That evening I wrote in my diary, "I've fallen in love with London." Born in America of English parents and always residing in America, I suddenly realized, with some surprise, that I was English too and London's past was part of my own. For me the charm of this great city lay in its history, and I saw it everywhere. The Roman wall crops out in many places, due to the Blitz that uncovered it and the City that restored it with so much care. Medieval London can still be seen in a number of places. When Londoners go to Hyde Park today to relax and rollerskate or play ball or listen to a band concert near the Serpentine, they are enjoying the same place that Henry the Eighth enjoyed when he hunted there. Shakespeare's London can be found in the places that escaped the Great Fire of 1666. The Staple Inn buildings in Holborn and a house at Cloth Fair have survived and look much the same as they did when he trod the boards. The George Inn in Southwark may have seen his patronage. "Twelfth Night" was first performed in the Great Hall of Middle Temple.

House at Cloth Fair

After the Fire, London was enriched by Christopher Wren's churches, amazingly beautiful buildings with spires that hold such magic today that the high rise moderns around and above them can't despoil them. At least for me they can't. The first church I attended in London was St. Clement Danes, the R.A.F. church. Before Wren rebuilt it after the Fire, it had many times been a part of London's tumultuous history. The resident chaplain told me the story of Queen Elizabeth's troops mounting a cannon in its tower, to fire upon the Earl of Essex in his nearby house. True or not, it adds quite a flavor to the history of this church. John Donne preached there. In the eighteenth century its parish register was a record of brilliant names, and you can see the place where Dr. Samuel Johnson sat in the north gallery. Today his statue is in the churchyard facing Fleet Street.

*Dick Whittington's Cat
on Highgate Hill*

All the churches have their own fascinating histories, but St. Clement Danes will always be my church.

London grew and expanded beyond the old City walls. Its history can be traced in the fronts of lovely Georgian houses, in the intriguing mews and stables, in the parks and squares, and the canals and railway stations. Modern developments bear historic names, reminders of the places they occupy. Victorian and nineteenth century London tell their own stories. Bus routes read like histories.

I wanted to record it all. Using the fine guide book that London Transport published, I did many sketches during that first visit. There were many more faces of London that Bob showed me, including a famous cat on Highgate Hill. Dick Whittington's stone cat forever crouches at the place where his master heard the bells of St. Mary-le-Bow calling him back to London town. Many of these sketches are in this book. My special project that time was to find the churches mentioned in the old English nursery rhyme about the bells of London. Attending St. Clement Danes gave me the idea for I remembered the verse, "Oranges and lemons say the bells of St. Clemens." My dad had taught me this old favorite of English children. St. Clement Danes still has an Oranges and Lemons Service every year. Fruits from Cyprus were given to the children when I was there. I managed to find and sketch all but one of those churches whose bells pealed in that nursery rhyme. When I returned home to Maine they formed part of a popular exhibit of my drawings at the University of Maine.

I came back to America determined to visit London again as soon as possible. Two years later we spent the summer in London. I continued my sketching, but this time I concentrated on the City, for which I'd formed a great affection. Bob had bought me a small paperback, the Everyman's Library edition of *The Survey of London*. It was originally published in 1598 by a Londoner named John Stow, and Elizabeth was his queen.

When I first began to read it I felt that John Stow and I had taken the same walks. I knew the places he described, the streets he travelled, the churches he wrote about. That summer of 1976 was London's hottest summer in many years. For me it was intensified by the excitement of trying to find John Stow's London.

He was buried in the church of St. Andrew Undershaft and his tomb is there, given by his wife soon after his death. It was restored in 1905 by the Merchant Taylors Company. John Stow had been admitted to the freedom of this company in 1547. One day that summer, toward the end of our stay I went down to St. Andrew Undershaft to pay my respects to John Stow. I found the main door to the church locked so I went around to the tiny church-yard where there was another door. But, there was a sign saying that church activities were cancelled because of fire. This was a bitter blow. The doorway was covered with canvas and there was a strong smell of smoke. It was lunch hour so no one was about. I poked my head through the canvas drop cloths and peered into the darkened church. Canvas draped walls and scaffolding and hard hats told the story. I knew where John's monument was supposed to be so I picked my way carefully along the north aisle to the very end and there I had my reward. In the smokey darkness, John Stow still sat at his desk. The ancient chronicler had survived the fire. I said a prayer of thankfulness and told him I'd be back another day.

Five years went by before we met again. It was January 1981 when we returned to London. During this visit I had the opportunity of attending his memorial service at St. Andrew Undershaft. In this finely restored church I watched the Lord Mayor present John with a new white quill pen, replacing the former black one. This is an impressive ceremony, held each year. The procession lists: "The Verger, The Churchwardens, The Common Councilmen, The Esquire, The Aldermanic Sheriff, The Aldermen of Aldgate Ward, The Lord Mayor, The Minister." The address was given by an Oxford don.

I got to know the City pretty well on this trip. I visited City Companies on their open days. These City Com- panies (sometimes called Livery Companies because of their unique attire peculiar to their trade or profession) are the descendents of the early merchant guilds. They have exercised great influence in the City since medieval times and they still do today. I attended church services such as the Spital Sermon at St. Lawrence Jewry. John Stow wrote about this sermon when it was preached at the Spital Cross in the yard of St. Mary Spital Hospital. I worked at the excellent Guildhall Library on the days when it was too cold or wet for outdoor sketching. There I read about Elizabethan London, and of course I found John Stow quoted everywhere.

Our wedding anniversary was in February and presents from my husband included the Oxford University Press

John Stow's tomb at
St. Andrew Undershaft

two-volume set of *A Survey of London* by John Stow and a delightful book of maps called *The A to Z of Elizabethan London* published by Henry Margary in association with the Guildhall Library. The two volumes of Stow, reprinted from the text of 1603, with introduction by Charles Lethbridge Kingsford, are fascinating and full of information. The ease of working with them has allowed me to balance my diary and sketches with John's writings. The book of maps helped me trace his steps as he walked about the City, recording the streets and lanes and everything in them. Of course there have been many places I have not found. I went looking for the site of Bethlehem Hospital (poignantly called "Bedlam") and found the Liverpool Street Station instead. I walked the length of Curtain Road one dark gray day looking for the site of "The Curtain," London's first theater, hoping to sketch a memory of the old playhouse. If there was a marker along Curtain Road I missed it. Another day I walked along the street called St. Mary Axe. I knew this street only through Gilbert and Sullivan's "The Sorcerer":

> If you want a Proud foe to "make tracks"
> If you'd melt a rich uncle in wax
> You've but to look in
> On our resident Djinn,
> Number seventy simmery Axe!

St. Mary Axe

Now I know it as a modern street of office buildings but there are plaques recalling two of John Stow's places, St. Augustine Papey and Bevis Marks. According to John, its strange name comes from a long vanished small church called St. Marie Virgin, St. Ursula, and the 11000 Virgins, also sometimes known as St. Marie Axe because of a sign of an axe nearby.

I returned to London in the autumn of 1984 by myself this time, since Bob's death the previous year. I was apprehensive for he had been my great support. I need not have been concerned. As I traveled through London to finish up my sketches, John Stow once again took me by the hand.

One of the high points in this visit was Lord Mayor's Day. I joined a small group of friends at St. Clement Danes to watch the procession along Fleet Street from the roof parapet of the church. The long parade ended at the gates of the Law Courts directly below us. When the Lord Mayor went into the Law Courts to be invested, we climbed down from our dizzying perch to have a picnic lunch at the back of the church. I shall always remember the view through the open door. Coaches, two or three hundred years old, pulled by handsome dappled grays and creamy white or ebony black horses, grooms steadying the fretful ones, and liverymen eating lunches packed in wicker baskets. I bought my souvenir program from one of the Blue Coats, students from the same school, Christ Church, that John wrote about.

Another day I took a bus over to Chelsea to find John Crosby's house on Danvers Street off Cheyne Walk. This is a house that once stood in Bishopsgate. It was moved, stone by stone, and rebuilt in Chelsea by the chartered Bank of India, Australia and China when they purchased the original site in 1903. John Stow described the house as "builded of stone and timber, verie large and beautiful." I found it to be all he said it was. Its great hall still has the original roof and oriel windows.

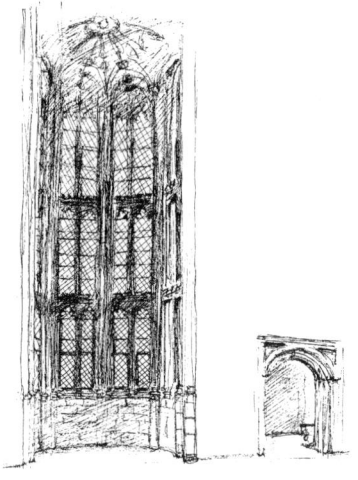

Crosby Hall

Three years later I stayed in London once more. This time was just to be a holiday, visiting family in Lancashire and friends in London. I planned without consulting John Stow. He was still there, enticing me on to find more of his favorite "cittie." I was fortunate this trip to be able to visit the Merchant Taylors' Hall where the obliging beadle showed me ancient parts of this famous hall. I found the original altar stone of the Augustine Friars Church and the effigy of Sir Nicholas Bacon in St. Paul's crypt. And one day I walked along Leadenhall Street and stopped to stare at the new Lloyd's building across the street from St. Andrew Undershaft and wondered how John would handle that description.

That was in 1987 and it was an indication of things to come. When I returned to London in 1990 I found the City in the midst of an enormous building boom. Everywhere I walked I saw new construction. The area around St. Andrew Undershaft along St. Mary Axe was an example. And what had happened to that great old Victorian pile, Liverpool Street Station? I had stayed away too long and I felt confused. Then I started to look for our special places (John's and mine). They were still there and many of them looked even more beautiful this time.

I was worried when I saw the lower level of Cleary Gardens closed off because of the excavations and the working cranes below it. However, the gardens still smelled earthy, the soil was rich, and there were hundreds of little pots of primroses scattered around the brickwork waiting to be planted where bulbs had just been dug up to make room for them.

Extra bonuses this trip were the churchyards of those two vanished churches, St. Pancrate and St. Benet Sherehog and the treasures I found at the Museum of London. Southwark was an adventure. The George Inn that I'd sketched in 1974 was more splendid now, its courtyard filled with greenery and outdoor tables. St. Thomas's tower still enchanted visitors although the Chapter House of Southwark Cathedral has moved away. Along the Thames to the west of the Cathedral I found more of John Stow's London, the little St. Mary Overy Dock, the breathtaking wall of the Bishop of Winchester's Palace and, down Clink Street, the Museum of the Clink. So much was going on here, I hated to leave.

In 1991 and 1992 I added a few more sketches of places I had missed on my previous visits and I spent more time just walking along old paths to make sure my maps were accurate.

1993 brought me back to London once again to be met with the tragic news of the bombing of the little church of St. Ethelburga. Apparently it will not be saved because the destruction was so great. When I designed this book I planned to use my sketch of St. Ethelburga on the cover. Let it now stand as a tribute to a small part of the City that has slipped away from us.

So London changes daily, yet so much remains the same. I hope I have captured John Stow's London in these sketches of the modern city. There is not room in one book to do all he wrote about. Much more awaits the curious visitor.

Note: This diary covers eight visits between 1974 and 1992. I have chosen to describe modern London ward by ward as John Stow did in *A Survey of London*. Because I've sketched London in a rather haphazard manner throughout the years, the diary entries are not chronological, but instead correspond to the wards under description. The marginal quotes and chapter headings are, of course, John Stow's own words and have been maintained in their original Elizabethan format except in the infrequent case when clarification was essential.

October 1994

DISCOVERING
ELIZABETHAN LONDON

The White Tower

1.

"Seeing that of euery these Wardes, I haue to say some-what, I will begin with **Portsoken** *warde, without Ealdgate. "*

Monday, June 21, 1976
My first visit to the Tower of London. I took a number 15 bus down to Aldgate and walked south along the Minories over to the Tower. There were long lines of visitors, most of them joining tour groups inside the Tower. I wanted to sketch so I started off by myself and came first to the White Tower. I got no further. This is the oldest part of the Tower of London, built in 1087 as a fortress and it is still a fortress today. I sketched a corner of it. It was strik-ingly beautiful as it curved skyward, all sparkling white and warm tones. Even the shiny black ravens posed for me. These birds were well cared for. They came from dif-ferent parts of the country and they all had names. According to an old superstition, six ravens must always be kept at the Tower or the Tower will fall!

When I left to walk back to the bus stop, I cut through Cooper's Row to the Minories and found a huge piece of the London Wall. There it stood, just part of the walls and buildings around there. I must go back to sketch it.

"Wherefore king *William,* for defence of this Citie, in place most daungerous, and open to the enemie, hauing taken downe the second Bulwarke in the east part of the wall, from the Thames builded this Tower, which was the great square Tower, now called the white tower, and hath beene since at diuerse times en-larged with other buildings adioyning, as shalbe shewed."

2

Tower of London

"Now of the parts therein, this is specially to be noted. First the East part of the Tower standeth there, then an Hospitall of Saint *Katherins* founded by *Maltilde* the Queene, wife to king *Stephen*, . . . *Helianor* the Queene wife to king *Edward* the first, a second foundresse, appointed there to be a Maister, three bretheren Chaplaines, and three Sisters, ten poore women, and six poore Clarkes."

Thursday, September 3, 1987

Left St. Margaret's Hotel at nine thirty to look for St. Katherine's Docks, a place I'd never visited. My map showed it to be near the Tower of London so I took the underground to Tower Hill. Plenty of signs pointed the way. Walking east along the path by the Tower moat, I felt rather nostalgic because this was where I'd first seen the Tower twelve years ago. I'd done a sketch of the walls from this very spot, but it was not a very good one. It occurred to me to try a watercolor from the same area. There were some workmen at the base of the great wall and I think I captured the atmosphere of this haunting place. I'd just about finished when the luncheon crowd came around so I moved on along the path eastward. I came through an underpass and out into the exciting world of St. Katherine's Docks, a modern development built on ancient foundations.

This is a series of enclosed docks harboring craft of all sorts from great working ships to tiny pleasure boats. I walked past a row of ships bearing such names as *Miscreant, Nore, Morayshire, La Chica, Czardus, Sans Fecht,* and *Dutch Pride*. The docks are ringed with towering buildings, banks, hotels, shopping areas, charming cottages, restaurants and pubs. Some of the old buildings have been restored. The Dickens Inn was once an eighteenth century brewery warehouse.

I was disappointed not to see any ships moving through the locks to the Thames. I did a sketch of a wall near the lockkeeper's office where a carved plaque

St. Katherine-by-the-Tower

showed the ancient name, "St. Katherine-by-the-Tower."
This was the site of St. Katherine's Hospital and Church,
moved from here in 1825 to make room for docks. The
hospital and church have been rebuilt near Regent's
Park.

Tuesday, October 8, 1991
Wandering today around favorite places, the Tower and
St. Katherine's Docks. I saw few visitors but lots of school
children, all very bright and lively. I found a spot sheltered from the wind yet in the sun so I could do a sketch
of the eastern end of the docks. One group of children
stopped to watch and a plump little boy with pink cheeks
and big eyes exclaimed "That's wicked!" All agreed with
him. A few years ago the word would have been
"fantastic."

St. Katherine's Docks

St. Botolph, Aldgate

"From Ealdgate East, lyeth a large streete, and high way, sometime replenished with few, but faire and comely buildings on the North side, whereof the first was the parrish Church of Saint *Buttolph*, in a large Cemitarie, or Churchyard. This Church hath beene lately new builded at the speciall charges of the Priors of the holy Trinitie."

Friday, April 26, 1974
Today I found St. Botolph Aldgate. This is one of three City churches called St. Botolph. This church was rebuilt by George Dance the Elder in 1744. The best view is from the Minories, not an ideal street to sketch from, but I perched on my tiny stool close to a wooden barricade sheltering some new construction and hoped no one would trip over me. I had quite an audience and was cheered on by two small girls who looked over my shoulder and said, "Oh, it's lovely!"

I took the drawing into the church and showed it to the vergeress. She looked longingly at it and said she wished they could have it printed. I felt guilty taking it home with me.

Tuesday, May 19, 1981

A rainy day, off and on. When I got to St. Botolph's Aldgate it was too wet to sketch outdoors so I went inside this church that I first sketched in 1974. An organ concert was in progress, so I sat in the balcony and thought of John Stow's remarks concerning the lofts of this church. The organ was quite near to me. I had a good view of the organist and the man who turned the pages for him, so I did a quick sketch while listening to Bach and Cleramboult and Rheinberger. Afterward I had a cup of tea with the people there and they were delighted to see my drawing. One of the women who worked nearby took it to her office and made some copies for the organist.

"The Parishioners of this parish being of late yeares mightily increased, the Church is pestered with loftes and seates for them."

Noon Concert at St. Botolph's

6

"... there was sometimes an Abbey of Nunnes of the order of Saint *Clare,* called the Minories, founded by *Edmund* Earle of Lancaster, Leycester and Darbie, brother to king *Edward* the first, in the yeare 1293 ... Neare adioyning to this Abbey on the South side thereof, was sometime a Farme belonging to the said Nunrie, at the which Farme I my selfe in my youth haue fetched many a halfe pennie worth of Milke, and neuer had lesse than three Ale pints for a half-pennie in the Sommer, nor lesse than one Ale quart for a halfe pennie in the Winter, always hote from the Kine, as the same was milked and strained."

Saturday, June 30, 1990
The Museum of London in the Barbican yielded some treasures today. I was especially drawn to a broken statue of a woman, missing her head and arms but still so gracefully posed that I couldn't help wanting to sketch her. When I read that she was from the nunnery of the Order of St. Clare I knew that I must sketch her. The placard said she was probably "Synagogue," representing the Jewish religion. So many times I've walked along the Minories from Aldgate to the Tower and passed St. Clare Street. The Abbey of St. Clare was in this neighborhood and John Stow bought milk at their farm. All this vanished long ago, but Synagogue still lives at the Museum of London and today she captured my imagination with her quiet and serene beauty.

Synagogue

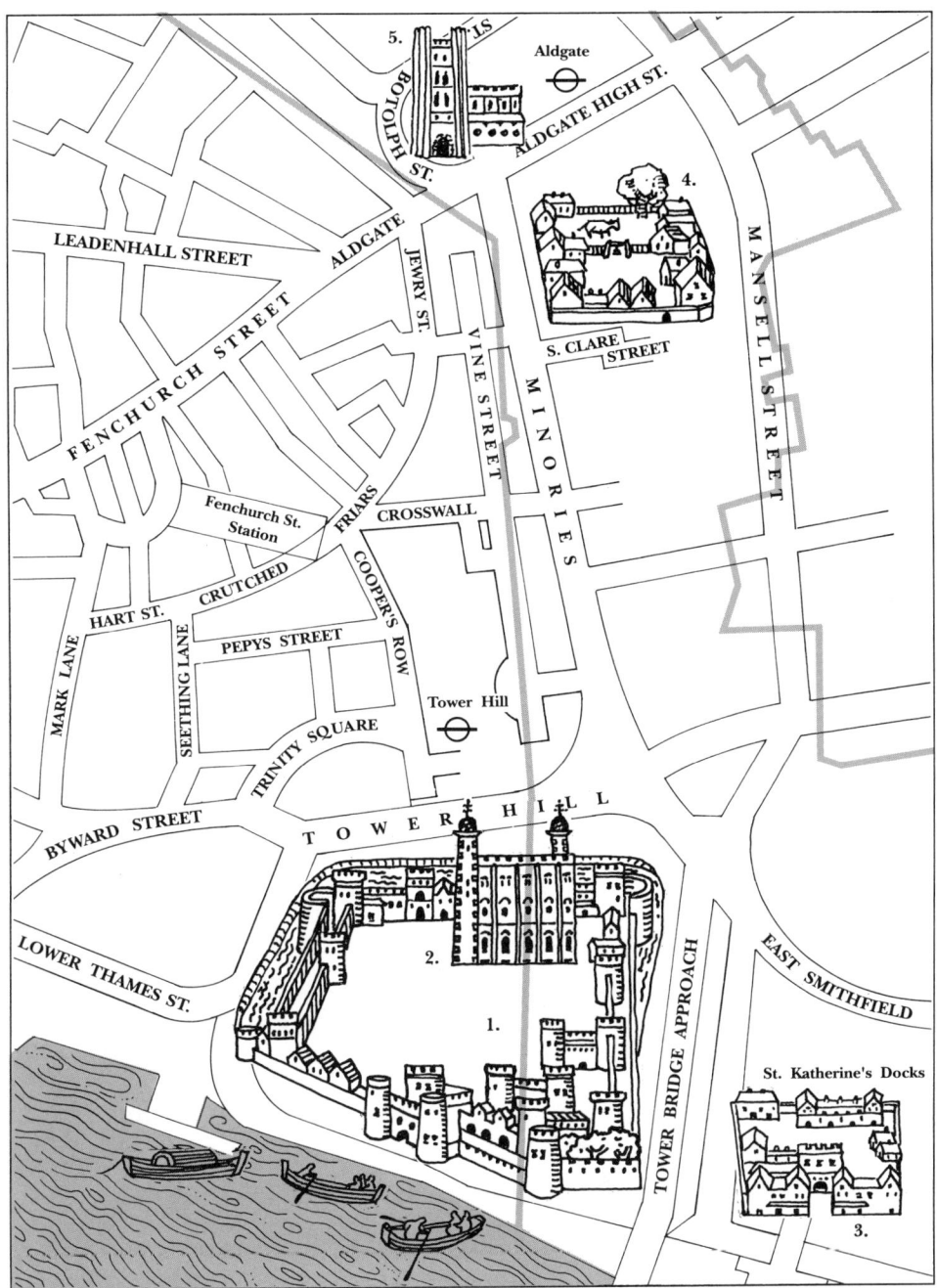

PORTESOKEN WARDE
1. Tower of London
2. The White Tower
3. St. Katherine-by-the-Tower
4. Abbey of St. Clare, called the Minories
5. Church of St. Botolph, Aldgate

2.

"The first Warde in the East parte of this cittie within the wall, is called Towerstreete ward, and extendeth along the riuer of Thames from the said Tower in the East, almost to Belinsgate in the West."

Friday, May 22, 1981
Such sunshine to wake up to! It's been wet for so long. I got off early to take advantage of the sun, but it was raining again when I came out of the tube at Tower Hill. I took shelter in the pavilion at Trinity Square and did a

watercolor of the site of the scaffold that John Stow wrote about. He described it in a very matter-of-fact manner, but I felt like weeping as I sketched this place, so beautiful on this fresh rainy May morning. A tree was in full bloom, dripping with alizarin crimson blossoms. Yellow flowers bordered the tiny brick pavement, marking the place where all hope ended for so many unfortunate people. The last execution there was in 1747. I felt annoyed at all the sightseers who came and looked and moved on with no interest whatever.

"From and without the Tower ditch West and by North, is the saide Tower hill. . . . Vpon this hill is alwayes readily prepared at the charges of the cittie a large Scaffolde and Gallowes of Timber, for the execution of such Traytors or Transgressors, as are deliuered out of the Tower, or otherwise to the Shiriffes of London by writ there to be executed."

Site of Scaffold, Tower Hill

10

"Now therefore to beginne at the East end of the streete, on the North side thereof is the fayre parish Church called Allhallows Barking, which standeth in a large, but sometime far larger cemitory or Churchyearde. On the north side whereof was sometime builded a fayre Chappell, founded by King *Richard* the first, some haue written that his heart was buried there vnder the high Altar."

Sunday, July 4, 1976

Happy Birthday, America! I celebrated today. First, service at St. Clement Danes and a long chat with Padre Thomas who was delighted with my plan to sketch All Hallows Barking by-the-Tower, a pre-fire church where William Penn was baptized and John Quincy Adams was married. It was extremely hot today, and a long wait for a bus coupled with a long walk searching for the church had me wilting by the time I got there. I found a side street off Byward that offered a good view of the tower and spire. There was even a spot on the sidewalk that had a tiny bit of shade from a garden area, so I sat there and did a watercolor. I'd been working about an hour when I looked up to see a tall man standing before me holding out a cup of tea. Said he was the bell ringer in the tower and had seen me and thought I might need to be refreshed this hot day. I was, in more ways than one. The tea gave me a much needed break and his thoughtfulness overwhelmed me.

After I finished I took my painting into the church to show him and all he said was, "You work fast, don't you!" No compliments there, but he took me up into the tower and told me about Pepys watching the Great Fire from there and showed me the small bells named for Penn and Adams. He even played the bells for me, just a little ring because he said it wasn't time to do them yet. It was too late by then to go down into the crypts where, as one Londoner told me, "all London's history can be seen." I'll do that another day.

When I came out of the church I walked north a bit and tried to imagine where that old chapel might have been, the one John Stow said was founded by Richard the First. Richard the Lion-hearted was one of my heroes years ago. When I was about twelve, knighthood was in flower for me.

All Hallows Barking by-the-Tower

12

St. Olave, Hart Street

Friday, May 8, 1981
Another warm day, sunshine and clouds but very
pleasant. Went down to the City, first stopping at Winsor
& Newton to pick up a couple of watercolor pads.
Wandered around a bit before I found Seething Lane,
still called by its corrupted name. I realized, somewhat
to my embarrassment, that I'd been here before. I'd
sketched All Hallows Barking from this very street in
1976. As I walked along, I wondered just where that
master spy of Elizabeth's, Sir Francis Walsingham, might
have lived, and also Essex. What a neighborhood this was!

Then I came to St. Olave, Hart Street. It's a pre-fire
church and absolutely fascinating. It was blitzed during

the war but restored with the original stone. The churchyard is a surprise. Dickens called it "the churchyard of St. Ghastly Grim." There was the gate with its skull and crossbones. Behind it, the small yard was elegant and cheerful, full of yellow daffodils. I sat there and did a watercolor of the sunken door and part of the ancient tower. A few people came to sit on the wooden benches along the wall and eat lunch. When they left I was alone again in the yard. I finished my sketch, but it was too late to work inside the church. I will have to go back later to do one of those effigies that John mentioned.

Wednesday, May 25, 1981
Stayed in our flat this morning waiting for the day to get brighter and warmer. It didn't, so I went back to St. Olave's to try a sketch of one of the monuments that John Stow mentioned. Inside the church it was almost too dark to see, but at least it was warm. Sir John and Dame Anne were in too much shadow, so I did Peter Chapone who was in a little better light, kneeling there on his pillow. I felt so sorry for him, coming all the way from Florence only to die of the plague in London. It was raining again when I left, and it matched my mood.

". . . Sydon lane, now corruptly called Sything lane, from Towerstreete vp North to Hart streete. In this Sidon lane diuers fayre and large houses are builded. . . . Sir *Frances Walsingham* Knight, Principal Secretary to the Queenes Maiastie that now is, was lodged there, and so was the Earle of Essex, &. At the North West corner of this lane, standeth a proper parish Church of Saint Olaue."

"Monumentes in this parrish Church of Saint Olaue bee these: . . . Sir *Iohn Radcliffe* Knight, 1568 And Dame *Anne* his wife, 1585 *Chapone* a Florentine Gentleman, 1582. . . . "

Peter Chapone, a Florentine gentleman, 1582

"This Church of Saint *Dun-stone* is called in the East, for difference from one other of the same name in the west: it is a fayre and large Church of an auncient building, and within a large Churchyarde: it hath a great parish of many rich Marchants and other occupiers of diuerse trades, namely Saltars and Iron-mongers."

Friday, June 7, 1974

I left early and came out of the Bank tube station before ten o'clock. I did two sketches and then I came upon St. Dunstan-in-the-East on Idol Lane. It took my breath away to discover it so suddenly. Wren's magnificent tower and spire rose into the blue sky above the lovely garden where the church had stood before the Blitz destroyed it. This was a Saxon church restored by St. Dunstan in 950 and burned in the Great Fire of 1666.

I sat in the garden and tried to put Wren's airy steeple on paper, with a view from almost directly beneath. I don't think I did it justice. People came in to sit awhile and I wondered if any of them knew the history of this place. Well, if they had lived through the Blitz, they knew some of it.

St. Dunstan-in-the-East

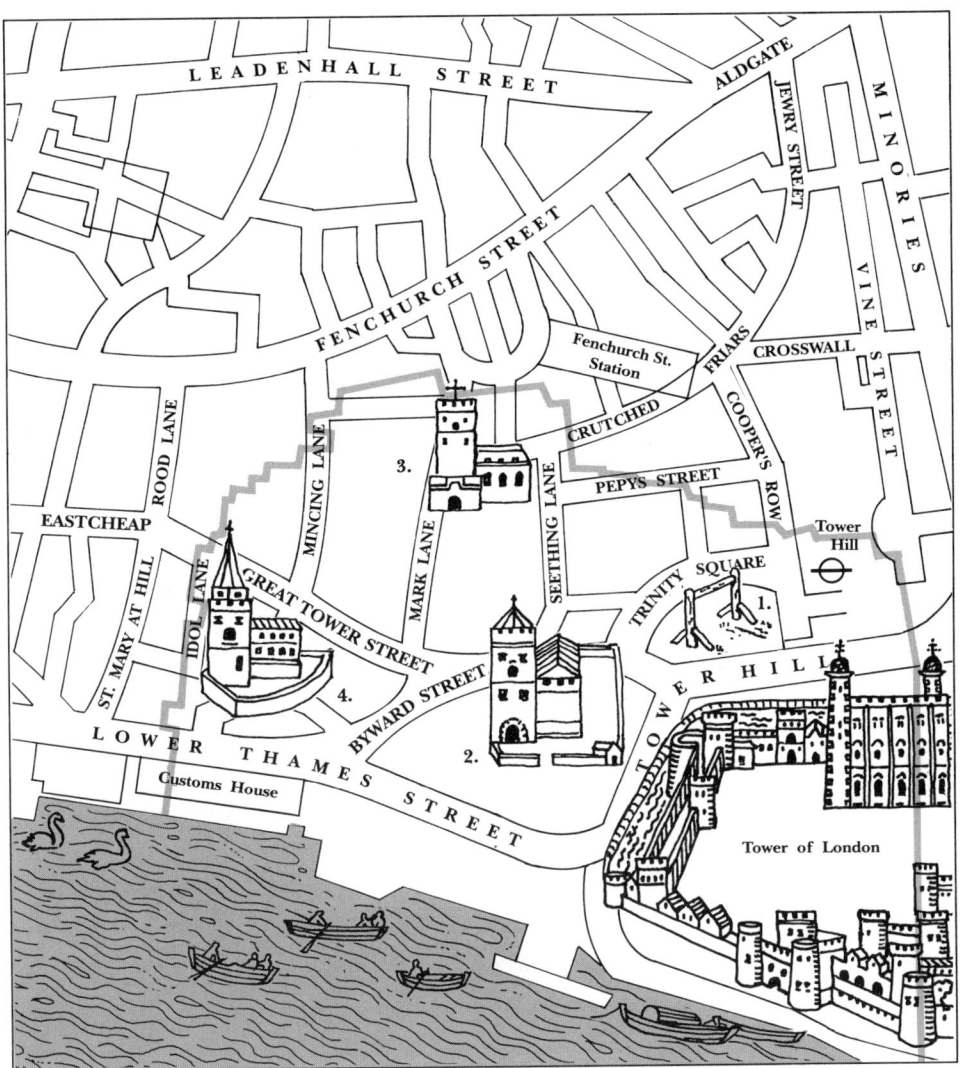

TOWER STREETE WARDE

1. Scaffold at Tower Hill
2. Church of All Hallows Barking-by-the-Tower
3. Church of St. Olave, Hart Street
4. Church of St. Dunstan-in-the-East

Aldgate

3.

"The second ward within the wall on the east part is called Aldgate ward, as taking name of the same Gate."

Saturday, May 30, 1981
Saturday's a good day to sketch, fewer people about. I took the bus to Aldgate to see if I could find the site of the old gate called Aldgate, one of the four original gates of the city. I was delighted to discover a plaque high up on a building along Aldgate which indicated that this was the site of the old gate. It was diagonally across from St. Botolph's Church so I sat in the churchyard and did a drawing of the area. This gate led to the east as the road still does. Chaucer once lived in this gatehouse. It was demolished in 1760.

"The next gate in the East is called *Aeldgate,* of the antiquitie or age thereof. This is one and the first of the foure principall gates, and also one of the seuen double gates, mentioned by *Fitzstephen.*"

18

*Nicholas Throckmorton at
St. Katherine Cree*

"The parish Church of S.
Katherine standeth in the
Cemitory of the late dissolued
priorie of the holy Trinitie,
and is therefore called S.
Katherine Christ Church. . . .
There bee the Monuments of
. . . Sir *Nicholas Throckmorton*
chiefe Butler of England, one
of the Chamberlaines of the
Exchequer, Ambassadour,
&c. 1570."

"Then is there a faire house,
. . . since possessed by Mis-
tresse *Cornewallies* . . . by the
gift of King *Henry* the eight,
in reward of fine puddings
(as was commonly sayd) by
hir made, wherewith she had
presented him."

Tuesday, May 19, 1981
Raining again but warmer, I visited St. Katherine Cree
Church, another pre-fire church and very beautiful. This
church was rebuilt in the early seventeenth century. I was
disappointed when I realized the narrow streets and tall
buildings surrounding St. Katherine's allowed no view at
all from the outside. Going inside I felt much better
when I found the perfect subject for a sketch, the elegant
monument to Sir Nicholas Throckmorton, one of Queen
Elizabeth's ambassadors. A famous street in the City is
named for him although the spelling is different,
Throgmorton Street. His daughter was maid of honor to
Elizabeth I. She was bold enough to marry Sir Walter
Raleigh without the great queen's consent. They were
both sent to the Tower for misbehaving. In spite of
Elizabeth, theirs was a happy marriage and it lasted until
his bitter end.

On the way home I walked along Leadenhall Street.
Somewhere along here, Sir Nicholas once lived. According to John Stow, he lived in a house that had belonged
to a woman who made puddings for King Henry VIII.
From studying old maps I think this house was probably
near Billiter Street.

Saturday, May 30, 1981

The corner of Leadenhall and Fenchurch Streets is the site of the ancient pump that John Stow wrote about, and a pump still exists there today. He told quite a story about an execution that he saw take place at the well. There was an evil man and an innocent victim involved. The man was Sir Stephen, curate of St. Katherine Cree Church, and the victim was the bailiff of Romford. Unjustly accused by Stephen, the bailiff met his death there. Today the Aldgate Pump is almost hidden by traffic barriers and I had to search for it. This was John's own neighborhood and, as I sketched, I kept thinking about the story he told of that poor bailiff.

"Soone after was there a Commotion of the Commons in Norfolke, Suffolke, Essex, and other shires . . . diuerse persons were apprehended and executed by Marshall Law, amongst the which the Baylife of Romfort in Essex was one, a man very well beloued: he was early in the Morning of *Marie Magdalens* day, then kept holy day, brought by the shiriffes of London, and the knight Marshall, to the Well within Aldgate, there to be executed vpon a Jebit set vp that Morning. . . . I heard the wordes of the prisoner, for he was executed vpon the pauement of my doore, where I then kept house."

Aldgate Pump

20

"At the North west corner of this warde in the said high streete, standeth the faire and beautifull parish Church of S. *Andrew* the Apostle, with an addition, to be knowne from other churches of that name, of the *Knape* or Vndershaft, and so called S. *Andrew Vndershaft*, because that of old time, eurie yeare on May day in the morning it was vsed, that a high or long shaft, or May-pole, was set vp there, in the midst of the street."

I finished the sketch and walked up Leadenhall Street to St. Andrew Undershaft where I did a watercolor of John Stow's own special church. Here he was buried and here, in his old age, James I gave him special permission to beg. A strange reward for his labors.

The tower of this pre-fire church is fifteenth century with a charming Victorian top. A class from Sir John Cass School was sketching here too, and the students kept coming to talk to me so the interruptions kept me there longer than usual and I got back to the flat rather late. It made for a long but satisfying day.

St. Andrew Undershaft

Saturday, September 8, 1984
Went down to Aldgate this morning. I stopped in to St. Botolph for a few moment's prayer before walking along the Minories to the Tower. I turned right onto Crosswall and then south toward the tower and came upon the London Wall I had found in 1976. But what a difference! Then it was part of the walls of old buildings being torn down, I could walk right up to it and touch it. Now it's the center of a dramatic setting. Walled off behind a sort of plaza with a sparkling fountain and stone benches, it is a lovely place to sit and relax or sketch. This is the third stop in "The London Wall Walk" following the original defensive wall of the City. The first Roman Wall was built in 200 A.D.

"These Romaines at their departure, tolde the Britaines playnely, that it was not for their ease or leisure to take vpon them any more such long and laborious iourneys for their defence, and therefore bad them practice the vse of armour and weapons. . . . they builded for them a Wall of harde stone from the west sea to the east sea. . . . This Wall they builded 8 foote thicke in breadth, and 12 foot in height."

London Wall at Cooper's Row

St. Katherine Coleman's churchyard

"Next . . . is the parish Church of saint *Katherine* called *Coleman*, which addition of *Coleman* was taken of a great Haw yard, or Garden, of olde time called *Coleman haw*."

Thursday, September 13, 1984
Today I finally found the site of another of John Stow's churches, St. Katherine Coleman. Now it is just a garden area near Fenchurch Street Station. Unfortunately, my first impression was at lunchtime and it was crowded with customers from a nearby pub. When most of them had left, I ventured in to try a sketch, despite the distraction of empty glasses left all over the paved courtyard. A man from the pub came in to clean up and tell me he'd be locking up soon. Apparently the pub takes care of this old churchyard.

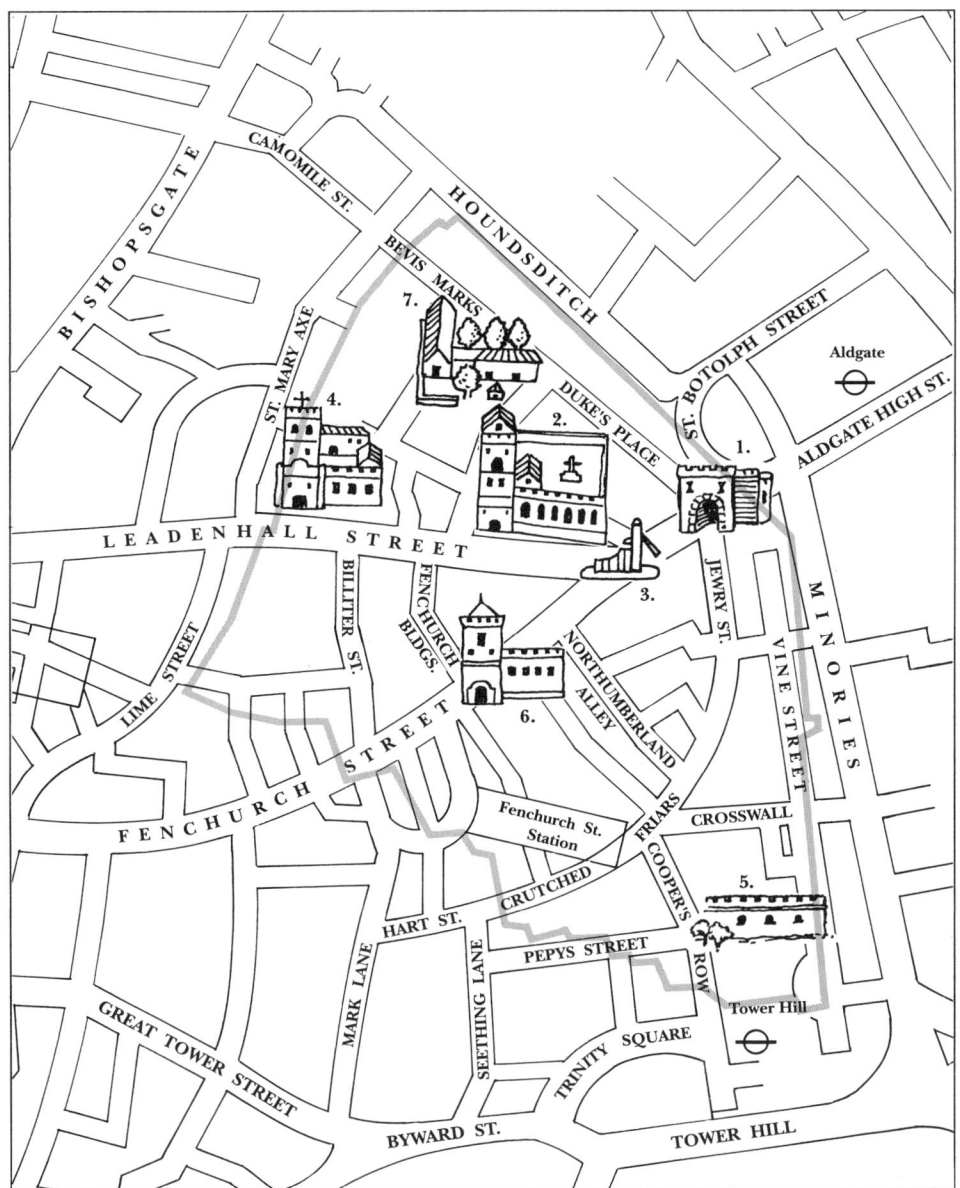

ALDGATE WARDE

1. Aldgate
2. St. Katherine Cree Church
3. Aldgate Pump
4. Church of St. Andrew Undershaft
5. London Wall at Cooper's Row
6. Church of St. Katherine Coleman
7. Bevis Markes
   Note: *See page xii.*

Leadenhall Market

4.

"The next is Limestreete warde, and taketh the name of Limestreete, of making or selling of Lime there (as is supposed)."

Friday, March 27, 1981

Sunny this morning so I left before ten o'clock to go to the City to find Lime Street. My head was filled with pictures of John Stow's Lime Street, especially the high wooden tower he wrote about. Well, there were high towers all right, but they were immense office buildings. The street was narrow and twisting with lots of construction going on and the sidewalks were boarded up tunnels. People were dashing about from one building to another. Activity everywhere. I know it was stupid of me to be so disappointed. There was probably a sketch there, but I couldn't see it. When I came to Leadenhall Street I turned left and headed for Leadenhall Market.

This was better, Leadenhall Market traces its history back to the early days of the fourteenth century and it is still doing the same business under the same name today. It was built on the site of a great Roman basilica (part of a mosaic pavement discovered there in 1806 is in the British Museum). In 1345 all poultry brought in to the City had to be marketed here. Dick Whittington and Simon Eyre are both part of its history. Destroyed by fire and rebuilt many times, the present market dates from 1881.

I went in the north gate at the end of the tiny Whittington Avenue. High above the delightful Victorian entrance I saw a clothesline of wash blowing in the wind. Perhaps there was one there in Tudor times too. The market is a fascinating place with its glass and iron roof arching over the colorful shops selling every kind of food imaginable, culinary items, housewares, gifts, arts and crafts, food and drink. It is a regular shopping center, and with such a flavor!

I could have stayed for hours, but I had work to do so I left by the west gate onto Gracechurch Street to try a sketch from across the street. I tucked myself into a

"In Limestreete are diuerse fayre houses for marchants and others. . . . *Richarde Wethell,* Marchant Tayler, builded a fayre house, with an high Tower, the seconde in number, and first of tymber, that euer I learned to haue beene builded to ouerlooke neighbours in this Citie."

"The vse of Leaden hall in my youth was thus: In a part of the North quadrant on the East side of the North gate, was the common beames for weighing of wooll, and other wares, as had beene accustomed: on the west side the gate was the scales to way meale: the other three sides were reserued for the most part to the making and resting of the pageants shewed at Midsommer in the watch."

"I haue seene a Quinten set vpon Cornehill, by the Leaden Hall, where the attendantes on the Lords of merrie Disports haue runne, and made great pastime, for he that hit not the brode end of the Quinten, was of all men laughed to scorne, and he that hit it full, if he rid not the faster, had a sound blowe in his necke, with a bagge full of sand hanged on the other end."

"And I haue reade that in the fourth yere of *Edward* the second . . . a Baker named *Iohn* of Stratforde, for making bread lesser then the Assise, was with a fooles whoode on his head, and loaues of bread about his necke, drawne on a Hurdle through the streets of this Citie."

corner of a doorway and did that entrance with its cock weathervanes, but I was much too close and there was too much traffic to be comfortable sketching there. These streets have always been crowded. Gracechurch, Leadenhall, Bishopsgate and Cornhill all meet here. In Elizabethan times this was where pageants and parades and games were held.

I bought a plump little chicken, a beautiful lettuce, and a loaf of Hovis bread to take home for dinner. When I bought the bread, I thought of that baker from Stratford that John wrote about.

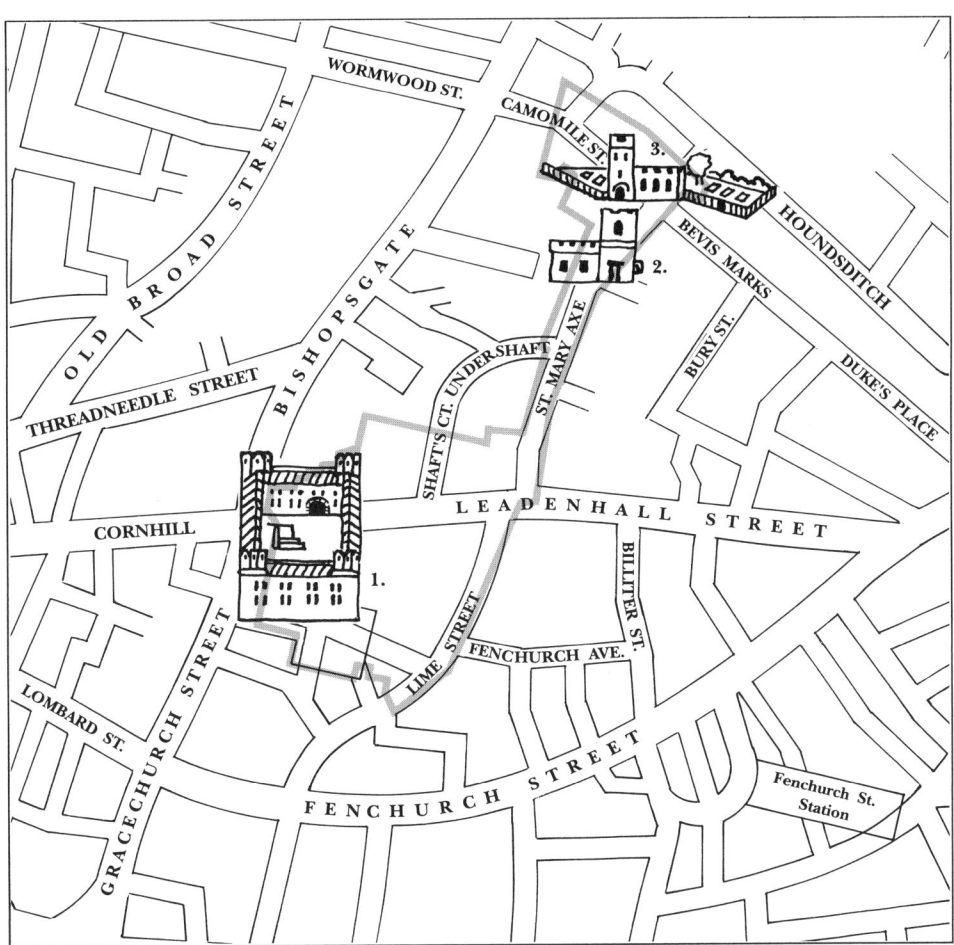

LIMESTREET WARDE

1. Leadenhall Market
2. Church of St. Mary at the Axe
3. Church of St. Augustine Papey
   Note: *See page xii.*

5.

"The next is Bishopsgate warde, whereof a parte is without the gate and of the suburbes from the barres by S. Mary Spittle, to Bishopsgate, and a part of Hounds ditch, almost halfe thereof, also without the wall is of the same Warde."

". . . the Parrish church of S. *Buttolph* without Bishopsgate in a fayre Church yearde, adioying to the Town ditch vpon the very banke thereof, but of olde time inclosed with a comely wall of bricke, lately repayred by Sir *William Allen* Mayor, in the yeare 1571, because he was borne in that parrish, where also he was buried."

Tuesday, October 16, 1984
A misty cool morning. I took the tube down to Bishopsgate to sketch St. Botolph, Bishopsgate. My first view of this church was in 1981. I had just walked down Old Broad Street to London Wall and suddenly I saw a shimmering reflection of a church tower in the dark glass facade of a modern office building. I turned the corner and there stood St. Botolph, a friendly looking red brick church in a charming garden with a pretty little brick schoolhouse in back. This is one of three churches dedicated to St. Botolph. Originally there were five, all of them at City gates. St. Botolph was an Anglo-Saxon abbot, the patron saint of travelers. John's church was outside

the City walls, today this eighteenth century church still stands on the same part of Houndsditch as the church that John knew, and there are still plenty of brick walls around. People who work and shop in this neighborhood come here to sit in the garden. There is usually a small group of unfortunates waiting for the pubs to open. One came over and watched me sketching for some time before he finally asked me for 40 pence. This took some of the joy from the morning. I never get used to it.

St. Botolph, Bishopsgate

"Next vnto this is the small Parish Church of Saint *Ethelburge* virgin, and from thence some small distance is a large court called little S. *Helens*, because it pertained to the Nuns of Saint *Helens*, and was their house."

Wednesday, July 7, 1976

Still hot, still no buses, so I took the tube to the City and ended up at St. Ethelburga the Virgin. John Stow barely mentions this church, but I love it. The smallest church in the City, St. Ethelburga was so hemmed in as to be almost lost along busy Bishopsgate. But what a relief to come inside this cool, dark interior from the bright heat and noise outside. The only sound is a clock ticking in the gallery. Through the verger's room at the back is the churchyard. It is a tiny lovely space surrounded by skyscraper neighbors. I'll always remember my first visit here two years ago when I asked the verger if I might go into the cloister garden. His reply, "Yes, but mind the bird," had me wondering if I'd heard him correctly until I went into the churchyard and saw a small brown pheasant moving jerkily around the brick arches.

I had to go back today to see if the bird was still there. She was, and so was the verger. He remembered me, "The old hen has a friend now. An alderman's wife brought in a cock so the hen would have company, but he has to be locked up until his wings are clipped. He took off for a fortnight and flew all around the banks here before they caught him at a nearby pub." The verger was in a chatty mood. Still, I managed to get a sketch of the hen in the cloister.

Cloister of St. Ethelburga

St. Ethelburga, Bishopsgate

Thursday, July 8, 1976
I wasn't too happy with the drawing I did yesterday, so I
went back again today. From across Bishopsgate there is
a perfect view of St. Ethelburga. John would have known
this facade with its fifteenth century window, but the
turret and weathervane are a later period. My sketch
came out quite well and I was glad that I'd tried one
more sketch of St. Ethelburga.

St. Helen, Bishopsgate

"In this court standeth the church of S. *Helen,* sometime a Priorie of blacke Nuns, and in the same a parish Church of Saint *Helen.*

This Priorie was founded before the raigne of *Henrie* the third. *William Basing* Deane of *paules* was the first founder . . . this Priorie . . . was surrendred the 25 of Nouember, the thirtie of *Henrie* the eight, the whole Church, the partition betwixt the Nuns Church, and the Parish Church being taken downe, remaineth now to the Parish, and is a faire Parish Church."

Palm Sunday, April 12, 1981
I first sketched St. Helen, Bishopsgate in 1974 when I was doing the churches in the nursery rhyme about the bells of London, "You owe me five shillings say the bells of St. Helen's." It is an amazing church, purely medieval, but far from a relic. There is a strong ministry going on in this church today. When I arrived, people were just leaving after the Palm Sunday service. I stayed long enough to do a drawing and put some color into it. The colors today were dark and somber. The past seemed to hover over St. Helen's in the unsettled sky, the bare branches of the trees just awakening from their winter's sleep, and the sharp wind sweeping by her ancient walls. Soon everyone left and I was alone until a young bobby came over to check me out. He nodded his approval and continued on his rounds.

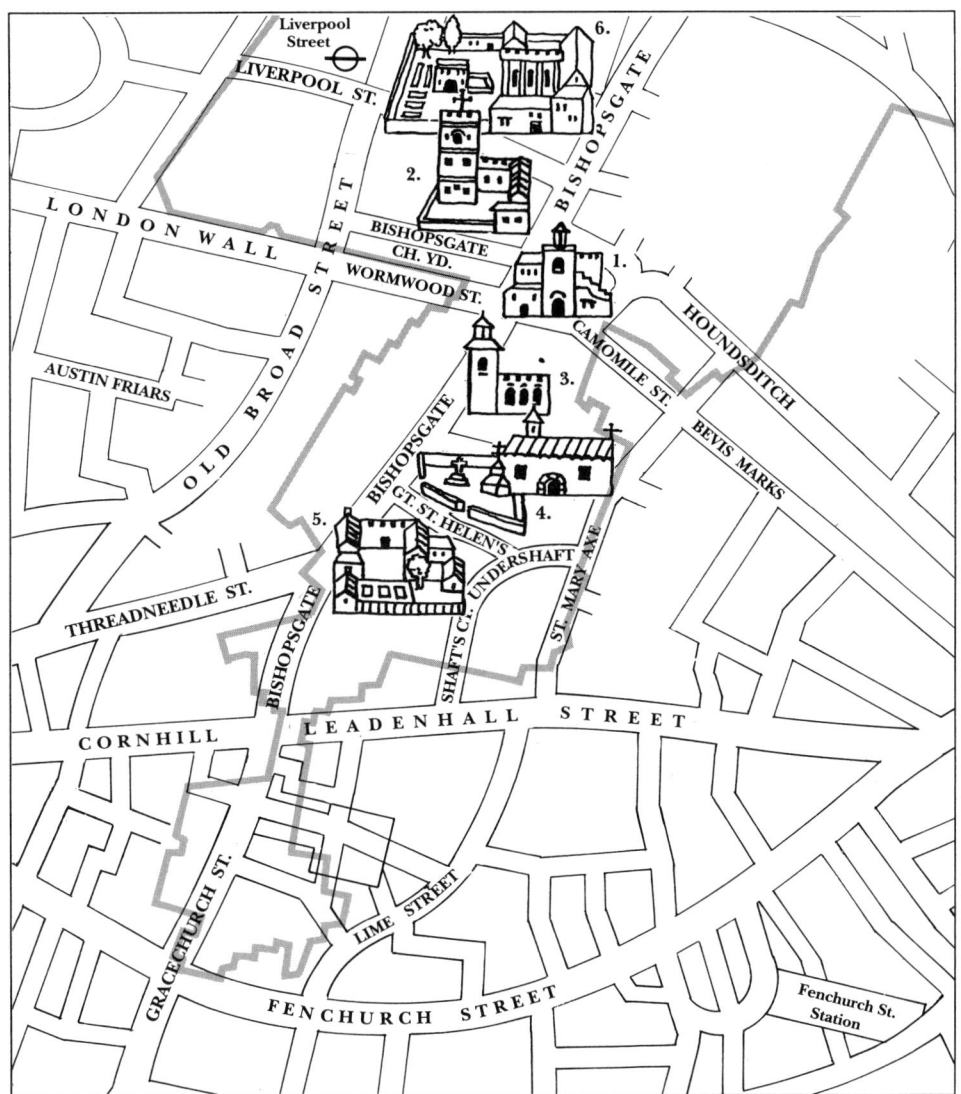

BISHOPSGATE WARDE

1. Bishopsgate
2. Church of St. Botolph, Bishopsgate
3. Church of St. Ethelburga, Bishopsgate
4. Church of St. Helen, Bishopsgate
5. Sir John Crosby's House
6. Hospital of St. Mary of Bethleham
   Note: *See page xii.*

6.

"The next is Brodestreete warde, which beginneth within Bishopsgate, from the water conduit westward on both the sides of the streete. . . . Then haue ye Brodestreete, whereof the ward taketh name."

Saturday, September 22, 1984

When the rain turned to sunshine I hurried down to the City to the street called London Wall, so named for the ancient wall that once ran along there. Here I found the church of All Hallows London Wall. The old maps called it All Hallows-in-theWall for it was actually built against the wall. I sat across the street where I had a view of the tower and the lovely restrained south wall of brown brick. The early church escaped the Fire and lasted until 1765, when George Dance the Younger rebuilt it. He was only twenty-four years old at the time. There is still ancient brickwork in the churchyard and the north wall of the church. All Hallows is now the headquarters of the Council for the Care of Churches. As I walked along London Wall after sketching, I passed an impressive building and was delighted to see that it was the new Carpenter's Hall, still on its original site.

". . . the parish church of Alhallowes in the wall, so called of standing close to the wal of the Citie. . . . On the other side of that streete amongest many proper houses possessed for the most part by Curriers is the Carpenters hall, which companie was incorporated in the 17 yeare of king *Edward* the fourth."

All Hallows, London Wall

Relic of Austin Friars Church

Saturday, October 6, 1984
Sunshine made this cool day bearable. I managed two drawings, Austin Friars Dutch Church and the Drapers' Garden on Throgmorton Avenue. I've been down to this Dutch Church before, it's a lovely area but with no view from outside the church. And the church seems to be always locked when I am there. Today was no different. This church has belonged to the Dutch people for a long time. It was bombed during the Blitz and the Sunday after its destruction, the Dutch flag was flown over the ruins. It's since been rebuilt.

Someday I hope I'll get in to see the relic of altar stone from the monk's church. Today I did a sketch of what may have been the base of a column from the old church, with the Austin Friars street sign in the background. The Friars' Monastery was here. Streets bearing the order's name were all around the area.

"The Friers Church . . . was in the yeare 1550 graunted to the Dutch Nation in London, to be their preaching place."

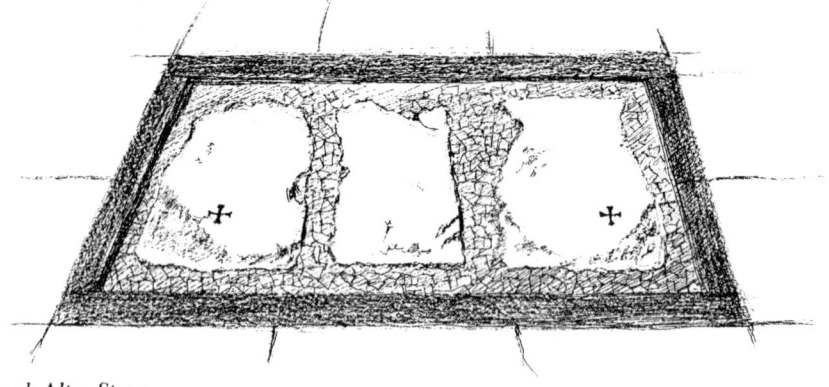

Dutch Church Altar Stone

"Then next haue ye the *Augustin* Friers Church, and Church yard, the entring there vnto, by a southgate, to the west Porch, a large Church, hauing a most fine spired steeple, small high, and streight, I haue not seene the like."

Monday, August 10, 1987
I stopped by the Dutch Church today and was ecstatic to find it open. I immediately pushed the doorbell. The verger answered and he didn't seem too happy to see a visitor. He'd been working downstairs on the floors. However, when I told him of my project he quickly led me to the original altar stone, the one from the old church. It set under glass in the floor under the communion table. Very handsomely done. He brought a chair for me to sit on while I did a drawing. It didn't take long before he was talking about the church, the tapestry and windows, and the order of service (which he translated for me from the Dutch). This is a simple, rather severe church, which creates a perfect setting for the beautiful African oak and the rich colors of the stained glass windows. And, oh yes, the verger said the stone I once sketched outside was from the original monks' church.

Saturday, October 6, 1984
The Austin Friars church sketch was a quick one so I had time to cross over to Throgmorton Avenue to try one of the Drapers' Garden. I sat on the steps of an office building across the street and sketched the garden, and while I was drawing I wondered if this might have once been part of John Stow's father's land. It was beautiful in the autumn sunshine. Drapers' Hall is on Throgmorton Avenue, an interesting short street with a gate at the far end, for pedestrians only. The Drapers have been in existence since 1180, and settled on this site in 1541 after Cromwell's execution.

"On the south side and at the West end of this Church, many fayre houses are builded, namely in Throgmorton streete, one very large and spacious . . . by *Thomas Cromwell* Maister of the kinges Iewell house. . . . My Father had a Garden there, and a house standing close to his south pale, this house they lowsed from the ground & bare vpon Rowlers into my Father's Garden 22 foot, ere my Father hear thereof, no warning was giuen him. . . . Thus much of mine owne knowledge haue I thought good to note, that the suddaine rising of some men, causeth them to forget themselues."

Draper's Hall

Merchant Taylors' Hall

"Some small distance from thence is the Merchant Taylors hal pertayning to the Guilde and fraternity of S. *Iohn Baptist,* time out of mind called of Taylors and linnen armourers of London, for I find that King *Edward* the first in the 28 of his raigne confirmed this Guild by the name of Taylors and linnen armourers, and also gaue to the brethren thereof authority euery yeare at midsommer to hold a feast, and to choose vnto them a gouernour, or Mayster with wardens."

Monday, August 10, 1987

It was almost three o'clock when I finished sketching in the Dutch Church. I was tired and hungry as I walked along the street called Austin Friars leading to Old Broad Street and the Royal Exchange. There I found a sandwich shop and revived enough to start looking for the Merchant Taylors' Hall. I found it behind a quietly impressive doorway along Threadneedle Street. John Stow belonged to the Merchant Taylors. I felt a bit nervous as I entered but I received a warm and friendly welcome from the beadle. He knew all about John Stow and showed me around the hall, which was being cleaned and renewed in preparation for their fall schedule. The old parts of this venerable building were fascinating but not very accessible for sketching, so I chose a corner of the garden. My guide assured me that there was a garden in this hall when John Stow was here. When I finished I was sorry to return to modern London. But a few hours later I was happy enough to be over on South Bank watching the Festival Ballet in Ashton's "Romeo and Juliet." It was a perfect ending to the day.

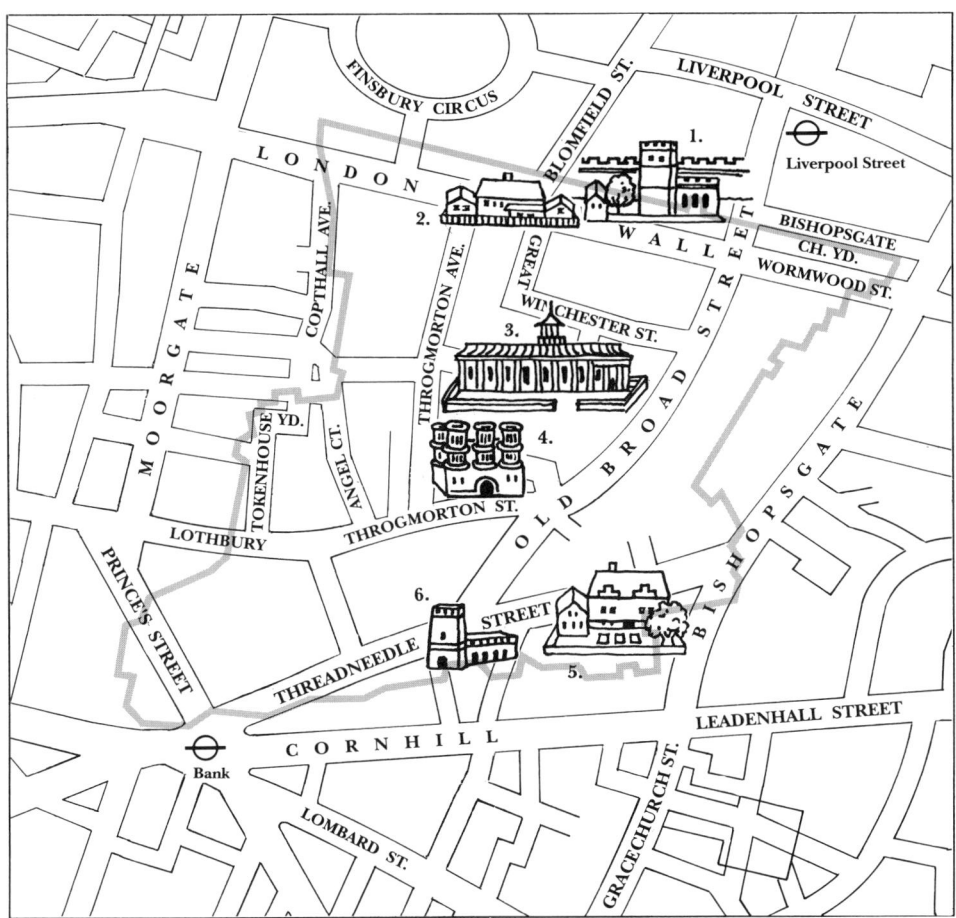

BRODESTREETE WARDE

1. Church of All Hallows, London Wall
2. Carpenters' Hall
3. Austin Friars Church (Dutch Church)
4. Drapers' Hall
5. Merchant Taylors' Hall
6. Church of St. Benet Fink
   Note: *See page 42.*

7.

"The next warde towards the south, is Cornehill warde, so called of a corne Market, time out of minde there holden."

Friday, April 10, 1981

Another warm lovely day. I got down to the City early. First I did the Royal Exchange, or the northeast corner of it where I found a place to sit in a small courtyard. Near me was a sign saying that this was the site of St. Benet Fink, a church that John Stow mentioned as being in Brodestreet ward. Wren rebuilt it after the Fire but it was demolished in 1843 to make room for the present Royal Exchange. This Royal Exchange is the third one on this site. Thomas Gresham, one of the City's great merchants and financiers, opened the first Exchange in 1566. When I finished my watercolor, a man who had walked by several times came over and asked if it was for sale. Felt pretty pleased with myself!

"In the yeare 1570 on the 23 of Ianuarie, the Queenes Maiestie, attended with her Nobilitie, came from her house at the Strand . . . to sir *Thomas Greshams* in Bishopsgate streete, where she dined. After dinner, her Maiestie returning through Cornehill, entered the Bursse on the southside, and after that she had viewed euery part thereof aboue the ground, . . . shee caused the same Bursse by an Herauld and a Trumpet, to be proclaimed the *Royal Exchange*, and so to be called from thenceforth, and not otherwise."

"Some distance West. . . is Finkes lane, so called of *Robert Finke*, and *Robert Finke* his sonne, *James Finke*, and *Rosamond Finke*. *Robert Finke* the elder new builded the parish Church of Saint *Bennet* commonly called *Fink* of the founder."

The Royal Exchange

Site of the Standard at Cornhill

Then I went over to Cornhill and Gracechurch Street to see if I could find the site of the Standard. This is a busy intersection, near Leadenhall Market and the church of St. Peter, Cornhill. I searched quite a while before I found a plaque, high up on the side of the southwest corner building that marked the site of the Standard. I sat diagonally across from it, in a sort of paved area with my back against a modern office building. This got me out of the traffic of this intensely busy place. It was busy here in John's day too. He wrote about the crowds that gathered at the Standard when it was a watering place. It was an amazing bit of city planning. Lead pipes brought water from the Thames up over the steeple of St. Magnus Church and down to the houses along nearby streets, ending here at the Standard. I sketched the corner building with St. Peter's spire behind it and the Gracechurch Street facade of Wren's church right next to it. People around me were meeting their friends and then rushing off to lunch. Again, one of them stopped to ask if he could buy my drawing. Londoners surely do love their City.

"First at the East ende thereof, in the middle of the high streete, and at the parting of foure wayes, haue ye a water standard, placed in the yeare 1582 in maner following. A certaine German named *Peter Morris*, hauing made an artificial Forcier . . . , conueyed Thames water in Pipes of Leade, ouer the steeple of Saint *Magnus* Church . . . vp to the northwest corner of Leaden hall, the highest ground of all the Citie, where the waste of the maine pipe rising into this standarde, (prouided at the charges of the Citie) with foure spoutes did at euery tyde runne . . . foure wayes, plentifully seruing to the commoditie of the inhabitants neare adioyning in their houses, and also cleansed the Chanels of the streete."

Gresham's Golden Grasshopper

"Then haue ye a faire Conduit, of sweete water, castellated in the middest of that warde and street. This Conduit was first builded of stone, in the yeare 1282 by *Henry Walles,* Maior of London, to be a prison for night walkers, and other suspicious persons, and was called the Tunne vpon Cornehill, because the same was builded somewhat in fashion of a Tunne standing on the one ende."

Sunday, May 24, 1981

After church I went down to the nearly deserted City to sketch one of the golden grasshoppers atop the Royal Exchange. The best view was from a doorway in a building at the corner of Cornhill and Birchin Lane. I did that pesky grasshopper three times before I got it right and I thought the sketch would take me only a few minutes. The grasshopper was on Sir Thomas Gresham's crest, and the one on the campanile is from the second Royal Exchange building. At this same corner is an interesting monument often overlooked. I was excited when I found it a few days ago. It is a pump that marks the place of one John wrote about. Ivy was growing out of it and a legend beside it read, "The well was discovered, much enlarged and this pump was erected in the year 1799 by the contributions of the Bank of England, the East India Company, the neighboring Fire Offices together with the bankers and traders of the ward of Cornhill."

The Tun at Cornhill

St. Peter, Gracechurch Street facade

Good Friday, April 12, 1974

Today I found St. Peter, Cornhill, the nursery rhyme church of "Pancakes and fritters say the bells of St. Peters." This is a Wren church built after the Fire destroyed the preceding one. It is supposed to be one of the oldest churches in the city. A brass tablet in the church gives 179 A.D. for its foundation by King Lucius. Whether true or not, St. Peter's is an ancient place. There's a seventeenth century organ there which was a favorite of Mendelssohn's, and the keyboard he used can still be seen. I sketched the facade along Gracechurch Street, a very noble wall of Wren's. Then I went around to Cornhill where I found a good view of the red brick tower and green copper dome with St. Peter's key high above. A man stopped to look, "I am so glad you are doing that. There aren't many of these churches left now."

"On the south side of this high streete is the Parish church of S. Peter vpon Cornehill, . . . there remayn-eth in this Church a table wherein it is written . . . that king *Lucius* founded the same church to be an Archbishops sea Metropolitane, & chief church of his kingdom, & that it so endured the space of 400 years, vnto the coming of *Augustin* the Monk."

St. Peter, Cornhill

St. Michael, Cornhill

"Then haue ye the parish Church of S. *Michaell* Tharchangel. . . . This hath beene a fayre and bewtifull Church, but of late yeares . . . greatly blemished by the building of fower Tenementes on the North side thereof towardes the highstreete, in place of a greene Churchyeard, whereby the Church is darkened and other wayes annoyed. . . buried there . . . *Thomas Stow* my Grandfather, about the yeare 1526, and *Thomas Stow* my father, 1559."

Saturday, October 20, 1984
I walked along old paths this afternoon. Very few people were about in the City's narrow lanes and quiet streets. I ended up at St. Michael, Cornhill. I've sketched this churchyard garden before, but today seemed the right time to do it again. A cold autumn day in the City, lonely and still. John and his father and grandfather seemed not that far away, and buildings were still crowded against the church.

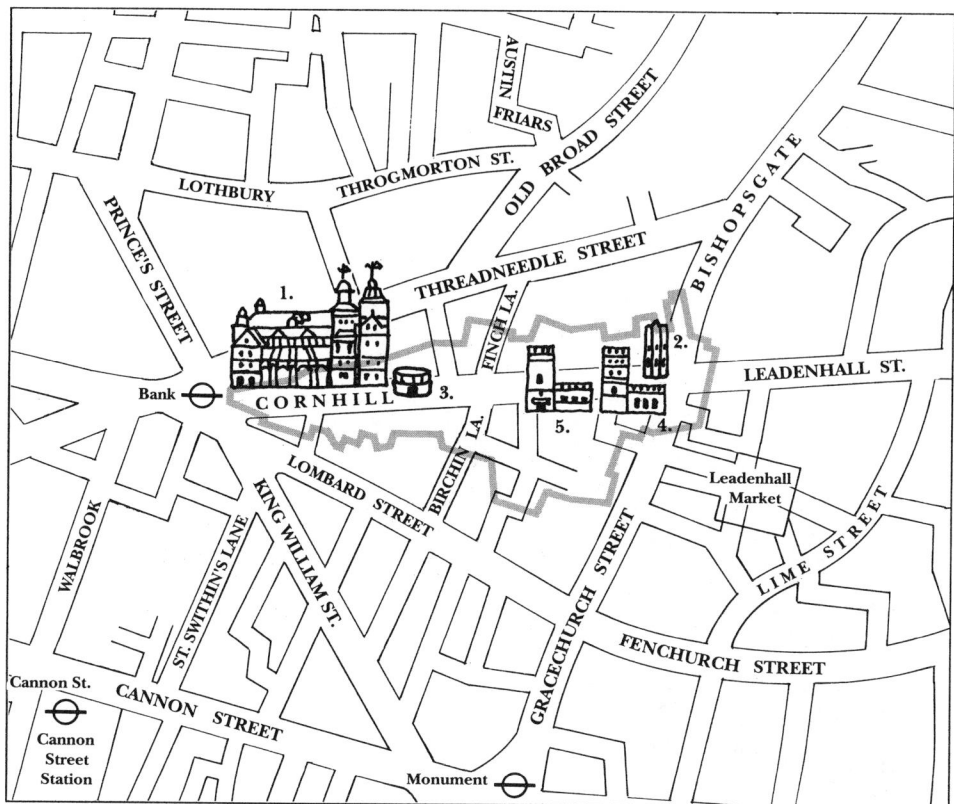

CORNEHILL WARDE
1. Royal Exchange
2. Standard at Cornhill
3. The Tun at Cornhill
4. Church of St. Peter, Cornhill
5. Church of St Michael, Cornhill

St. Gabriel's Churchyard

8.

"Langborne warde, so called of a long borne of sweet water, which of old time breaking out into Fenchurch streete, runne downe the same streete."

Friday, May 8, 1981

"In the midst of this streete standeth a small parish Church called S. *Gabriel* Fenchurch, corruptly Fan Church."

Walked around the Fenchurch area today and almost by chance I came to Fen Court. I realized that I'd been here before on some of my wanderings. Each time it enchants me, so today I sat down on one of the stone benches and did a drawing. This small courtyard is filled with plants and trees. A light, bright breathing space amidst the tall City buildings, this is the churchyard of St. Gabriel Fenchurch, a church destroyed in the Great Fire and not rebuilt. Its parish was united with St. Margaret Pattens.

Sunday, May 24, 1981

After sketching in the Royal Exchange area I walked over to St. Edmund, King and Martyr, another church rebuilt by Wren after the Fire. I sketched it from the back, sitting in George Yard. The stone tower has a lead steeple and it must have been an impressive sight when it had Wren's twelve flaming stone urns climbing its sides, but even now it is strong and splendid as seen from George Yard below. This yard, almost deserted today, was once the church-yard of All Hallows, Lombard Street, another Wren church. It was demolished in 1938 and its tower removed to Twickenham. Close by here was the George, an inn known to John Stow. Chaucer knew it too and after the Fire it became the George and Vulture of Mr. Pickwick fame. It is still there.

"Next to this is the parish church of S. *Edmond* the king and Martyr in Lombard streete, by the south corner of Birchouer lane.

This church is also called S. *Edmond* Grasse church, because the said Grasse Market came downe so low."

"In Lombard streete is one faire Parish church, called Alhallowes Grasse church in Lombard streete."

"Next is a common Osterie for trauellers, called the George, of such a signe."

St. Edmund, King and Martyr

Tower of All Hallows, Staining

Friday, September 7, 1984

It's taken me quite a while to find the tower of All Hallows Staining but I finally found it today on Mark Lane right across the street from Fenchurch Street Station. A church on this site was first mentioned in 1170. I sat in the tiny churchyard with my back to Mark Lane. There was a steady stream of people rushing by and at first this was distracting, the street was so close to me. But soon this old tower took over and I became engrossed in the ancient walls. With all the new construction, this tower seemed to be the only permanent building around. The church John Stow knew collapsed in the seventeenth century but was rebuilt and lasted until 1870, when all but the tower was demolished. It was locked today and I was disappointed because there is a tiny Norman crypt in there. It is a relic of the old Hermitage of St. James-in-the-Wall in Farringdon Ward Within that John Stow described.

Just before I finished my watercolor, one of the people hurrying along the street stopped to ask about the tower. He said he passed by here every day but had never noticed it before! He must have come from the suburbs. He couldn't have been a Londoner.

"On the Southside of this ward, somewhat within Mart lane, haue yee the Parish Church of Alhallowes, commonly called Stane Church (as may bee supposed) for a difference from other Churches of that name in this Citie which of old time were builded of timber, and since were builded of stone."

". . . an Hermitage, or Chappell of saint *James*, called in the wal, neare Crepplegate: it belonged to the Abbey and Couent of Garadon as appeareth by a Recorde, the 27 of *Edward* the first."

Martin Bowes Memorial,
St. Mary Woolnoth

"Then is there in the high streete a proper parish Church of Saint *Marie* Woolnoth, of the Natiuitie, the reason of which name I haue not yet learned. . . . Sir *Martin Bowes* Maior, buried about 1569 he gaue lands for the discharge of that Langborn ward, of all fifteenes to be granted to the king by Parliament."

Wednesday, October 3, 1984

St. Mary Woolnoth is a Hawksmore church near the Bank. Today being rather cold and damp, I thought I'd see what I could find to sketch inside the church. I was in luck for I found the memorial of Martin Bowes, the same Martin Bowes that John Stow mentioned. I was elated to see a glass case containing his helmet, gauntlets and spurs. It was quiet and warm in the church and I had just settled down in front of the case to do a drawing when the rector came over to say how happy he was to see me doing this memorial and would I like a cup of coffee. Before he left he told me to be sure to see the Bowes banner hanging in the back of the church. I did find it but it was too dark to sketch there. I could barely see the swan centered on the ancient color. The Goldsmiths Company keeps up this memorial to one of their illustrious members of the Elizabethan age.

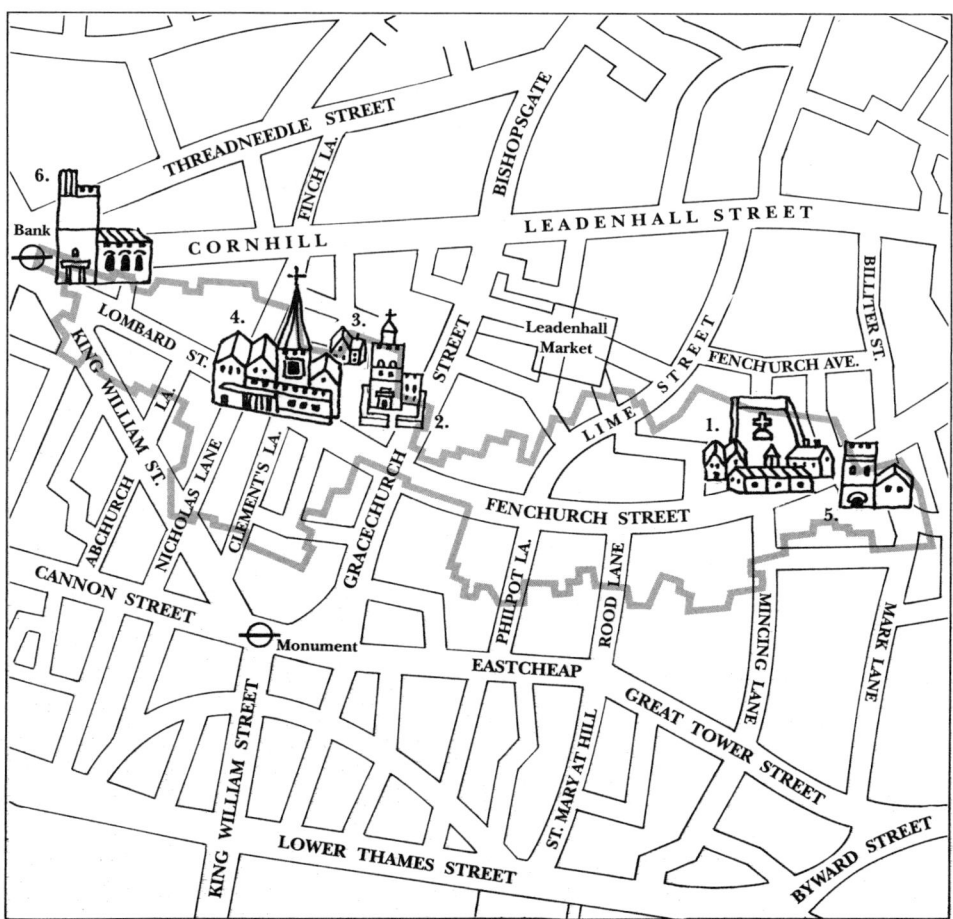

LANGBORNE WARDE

1. Church of St. Gabriel Fenchurch
2. All Hallows Grasse Church in Lombard Street
3. The George
4. Church of St. Edmund, King and Martyr
5. All Hallows, Staining Church
6. St. Marie Woolnoth Church

9.

"Billinsgate Ward, beginneth at the west ende of Towerstreete warde in Thames streete about Smarts Key, and runneth downe along that streete on the southside to saint Magnus Church at the Bridge foote."

Friday, June 7, 1974

I sketched Billingsgate this morning. This old fish market is now in its last days. All over this area buildings were shorn of facades, their insides hanging in plaster dust

and snarled and twisted wires. The deep excavations here revealed artifacts of London's past. People stopped to look through barricades to watch the treasure hunters below. Billingsgate itself still stands, with its red crosses and green arches and golden fish weathervanes and Britannia still rules over all. This market has carried on in the same place as John Stow's market. But it is soon to be closed and I felt as if I were sketching a death mask. A man stopped to beg me to sell him my drawing. I think he felt the same way I do.

"The next is Belinsgate whereof the whole warde taketh name, the which . . . is at this present a large Water-gate, Port or Harbrough for shippes and boats, commonly arriuing there with fish, both fresh and salt, shell fishes, salt, Orenges, Onions, and other fruits and rootes, wheate, Rie, and graine of diuers sort for seruice of the Citie, and the parts of this Realme adioying."

Billingsgate Market

St. Mary-at-Hill,
unfinished sketch

"In this saint *Marie* hill lane is the faire parish church of saint *Mary* called on the hill, because of the ascent from Billinsgate."

Thursday, September 18, 1984

I found St. Mary-at-Hill open today, the first time this has happened to me. This beautiful church, half hidden between Lovat Lane and St. Mary-at-Hill, seems to be open only at midday. I sat in one of the deep box pews and tried a drawing of the inside, but I did not get it finished before quarter past one when the Eucharist started. The men at this service were very pleasant and urged me to continue, but I left, thinking to come back another day to finish it. This church was rebuilt by Christopher Wren after it was burnt in the Fire. Again restored in 1787, it has a radiant interior today. The pulpit was repaired by W. Gibbs Rogers after another fire, but I've read that it is very much like the work of the Wren period.

St. Mary-at-Hill's churchyard

Tuesday, November 13, 1984

It was pretty cool today. Went back to St. Mary-at-Hill to finish my drawing. This time I got there by noon but the church was closed again. I decided to sit in the tiny churchyard and do the wall of the church. It was rather forlorn this November day. As I sketched I thought about Thomas Becket who may have walked along this very churchyard, for he was once a parson at St. Mary-at-Hill.

"This *Thomas*, surnamed *Becket*, borne in London, brought vp in the Priorie of Marton, student at Paris, became the Shiriffes Clarke of London for a time, then person of Saint Marie hill . . . was made Chancellor of England, and Archbishop of Canterburie, &c."

St. Margaret Pattens

"One other lane called *S. Margaret Pattens,* because of olde time Pattens were there vsually made and sold: but of latter time this is called Roode lane, of a Roode there placed, in the Churchyeard of Saint *Margaret,* whilest the olde Church was taken downe, and againe newly builded, during which time the oblations made to this Roode, were imployed towardes building of the Church."

Monday, April 29, 1974

After a sandwich and a cup of tea at a shop near the Monument, I went over to sketch St. Margaret Pattens, Rood Lane. I tried it from about halfway up the street called St. Mary-at-Hill. The simple lead spire of St. Margaret's is one of Wren's tallest steeples and the only one remaining today that is wood covered with lead. This church has a long history, starting more than 900 years ago. One reason given for its odd name is that a patten was a kind of shoe made near here. It had a wooden sole with leather straps mounted on a large iron ring to raise the wearer up out of mud. Pattens were very noisy and there is still a sign in this church that says, "leave pattens before entering." The Pattenmakers Company is associated with St. Margaret's.

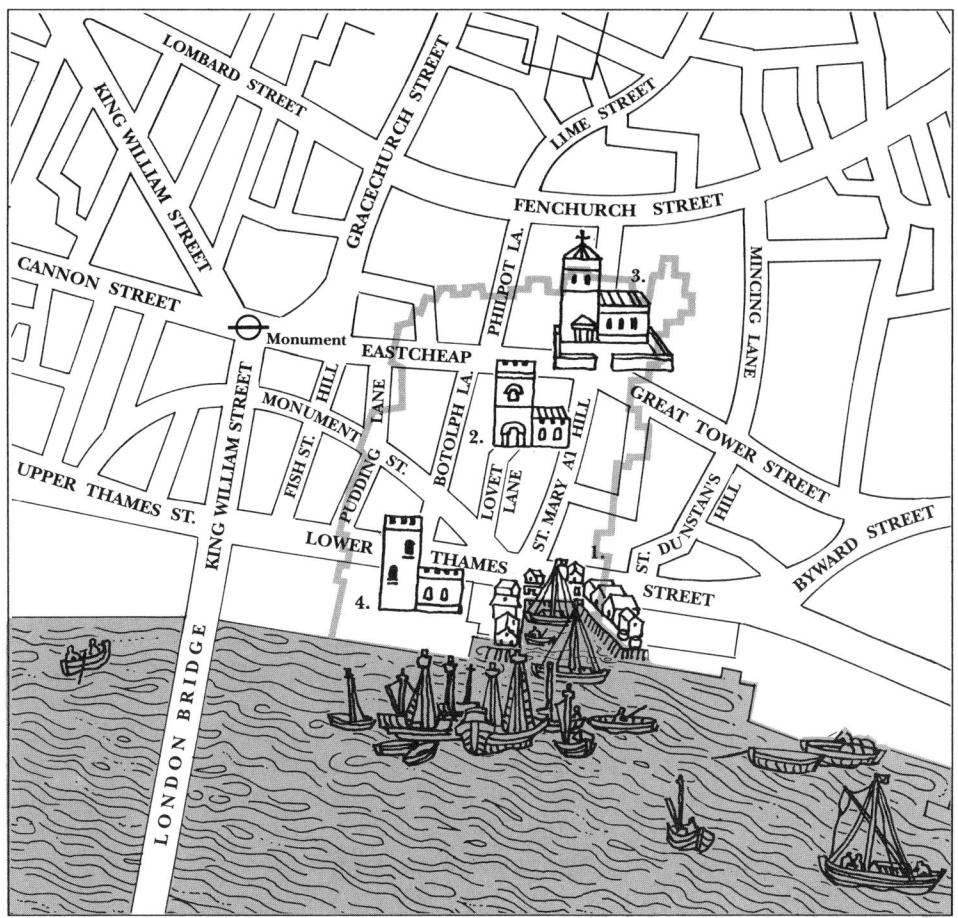

BILLINSGATE WARDE

1. Billingsgate Market
2. St. Mary-at-Hill Church
3. St. Margaret Pattens Church
4. Church of St. Botolph, Billingsgate

10.

"Bridgeward within, so called of London Bridge, which Bridge is a principall part of that ward."

"This bridge ouer the said riuer of *Thames,* I affirme, as in other my descriptions, that it is a worke verie rare, hauing with the draw bridge 20 Arches made of squared stone, of height 60 foote . . . compact and ioyned togither with vaults and cellers, vpon both sides be houses builded, so that it seemeth rather a continuall streete then a Bridge: for the fortifying whereof against the incessant assaults of the riuer, it hath ouerseers and officers."

Friday, September 7, 1984

I walked over London Bridge to Guy's Hospital in Southwark this afternoon. This bridge was opened by Her Majesty the Queen in 1973. There have been many bridges here since Saxon times. According to Stow, his bridge was made of stone and built in 1176. Repaired many times, it lasted until 1831 when a new bridge replaced it. The bridge I walked across today, a little more to the east of John's bridge, was a far cry from the one he knew, but I think the atmosphere around it was much the same. It was a gray misty afternoon. The sky and the Thames and the buildings along the banks were washed in pale lamp black. The river moved slowly. I stopped to look over the rail and watch three small brown ducks swim downstream towards St. Magnus the Martyr (a beautiful church now almost completely hidden by the tall buildings around it.) At Guy's Hospital I found the arched alcove that was once part of the old London Bridge around 1760. This lovely relic sits in one of Guy's two inner courtyards. The hospital, founded in 1722, purchased this alcove in 1861 "for 10 guineas as a shelter for convalescing patients."

Saturday, June 30, 1990

Another of my sketches from the Museum of London's splendid medieval gallery was a relic of the first London Bridge. This was a stone bracket found in the Thames. It had a carved head, almost worn smooth now, and thought to be of Thomas Becket. In the same case with this bracket was a piece of piling, also from the Thames, that came from the first bridge.

*Stone bracket from London Bridge
at the Museum of London*

*Arched alcove of the old London Bridge
at Guy's Hospital*

Tower of St. Magnus the Martyr

Sunday, September 23, 1985

The Church of St. Magnus the Martyr is not easy to see, being so crowded by tall neighbors. The church booklet says that churches have stood on this site for over a thousand years, welcoming visitors who cross the river to the City. Wren rebuilt this church after the Fire, but only the lower walls of the old church remain today. I once tried to find some sign of Henry Yevele's monument in there but I was disappointed. This afternoon I found a place across the street, close by some new construction, and settled in to draw the base of the tower. One of Wren's finest towers, it rises on arches over a tiny church-yard where a footpath used to run to the old London Bridge. I was intent on capturing these old arches when I heard a disturbing "splat" and a raindrop appeared on my drawing. I barely got my umbrella up in time. I continued on, holding the umbrella in my left hand. People going by gave me a few quick glances but I finished the sketch before I got too wet.

Sunday, September 9, 1984
An impressive service at St. Clement Danes this morning with visiting members of the Polish Air Force placing a wreath on their handsome memorial. After the service I took a number 513 bus down to St. Magnus the Martyr, not far from London Bridge. I strolled around a while and came to the back of St. Magnus. There was a charm-ing garden courtyard there in front of a very modern office building. From there I did a sketch of the east end of this old church because the proportions were intrigu-ing. I think I may have been sitting very near to the place where another old church once stood, St. Botolph, Billingsgate (in Billingsgate Ward). Of course St. Boltolph was right in the path of that awful fire in 1666. It was not rebuilt.

"On the East side of this Bridge warde, haue yee the fayre Parrish Church of S. *Magnus,* in the which church haue beene buried many men of good Worship. . . . I find . . . *Henry Yeuele* Freemason to *E.* 3 *Richard the* 2 & *Henry the* 4 who deceased 1400 his Mon-ument yet remayneth."

"Next is the parish Church of Saint *Buttolphs,* a proper church, and hath had many fayre monuments therein, now defaced and gone."

St. Magnus the Martyr from the east

Wednesday, August 18, 1976

I had such a busy morning sketching at Southwark that I didn't have much energy left when I got over to Fish Street Hill. However I managed a quick sketch of the Monument. This column commemorates the Great Fire that started September 2, 1666, and burned four fifths of the City in four days. Designed by Wren and the City Surveyor, Robert Hooke, the monument soars into the sky for 202 feet. That is the exact distance from the column to the place of the baker's shop in Pudding Lane where the fire started. The monument is built on the site of St. Margaret, Fish Street Hill, an ancient church that was swept into ashes that morning of September 2, 1666.

"Then is the parrish Church of S. *Margaret* on Fishstreete hill, a proper Church, but monumentes it hath none."

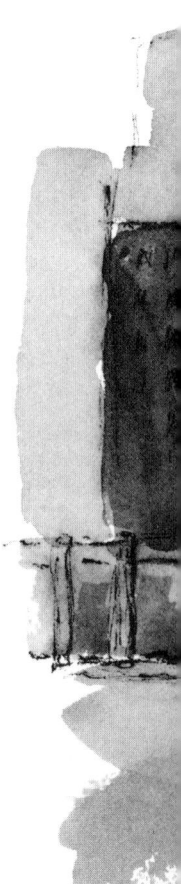

The Monument, Fish Street Hill

Friday, June 29, 1990

Lots of walking today, renewing the excitement I felt when I first sketched John's landmarks. I ended up crossing London Bridge. As I passed Fishmongers' Hall I thought, "I should really sketch this place," but I've never found a good view except from the bridge and I was too weary to stand there and try that. I walked over to the

Fishmongers' Hall

"On the South side of Thames streete, about the midway betwixt the bridge foote, and Ebgate lane, standeth the Fishmongers hall, and diuerse other fair houses for marchants.

These Fishmongers were sometimes of two seuerall companies, to wit, Stocke-fishmongers, and Saltfish-mongers, of whose antiquitie I reade, that by the name Fishmongers of London, they were for forestalling, &c. con-tarie to the lawes and con-stitutions of the Citie, fined to the king at 500 markes, the 18 of king *Edward* the first. More, that the said Fish-mongers, hearing of the great victorie obtained by the same king against the Scots, in the 26 of his raigne, made a triumphant and solemne shew through the Citie, with diuerse Pageants, and more then 1000 horsemen, &c."

Cathedral and around to Thame side to look at the river. There, across the Thames waiting for me to do a sketch, was the classic design of Fishmongers' Hall.

The Fishmongers are the fourth of the twelve great City Companies and one of the oldest. Their hall was destroyed in the Great Fire and rebuilt soon after. This hall was built in 1834 on the original site. I was lucky enough to visit the hall in 1981, and I remember the magnificent Waterford chandeliers and especially the ceilings, staircases, and halls, which were most impressive. The preserved manuscripts and rate books there gave glimpses into a rich past. And there is a wooden statue of Sir William Walworth, mayor of London, who killed the rebel Wat Tyler in 1381. Even the dagger that did the deed was there!

I made a bad start and had to sketched it twice before I got what I wanted. By the time I'd finished, the somber colors and tints of the riverside carried the ancient atmosphere right into my watercolor.

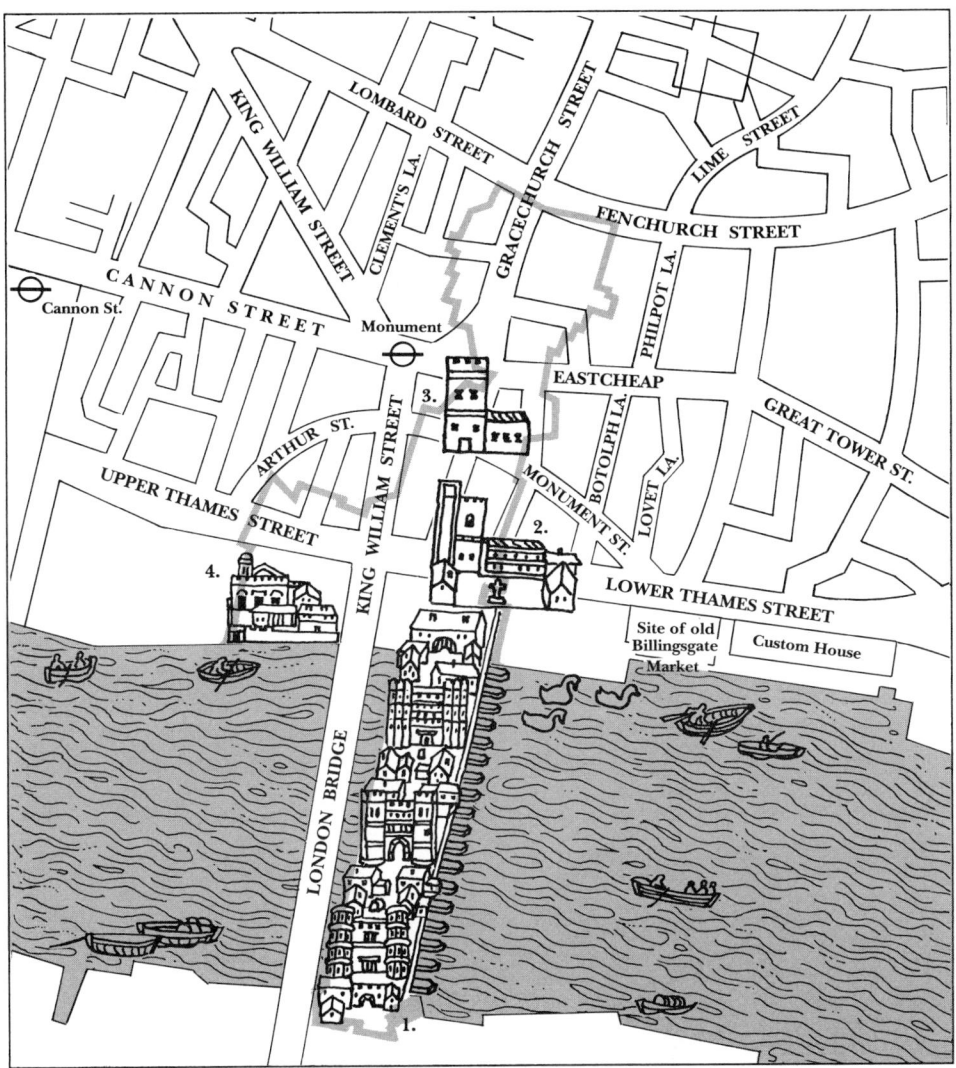

BRIDGEWARDE WITHIN

1. London Bridge
2. Church of St. Magnus the Martyr
3. Church of St. Margaret on Fish Street Hill
4. Fishmongers' Hall

11.

"Candlewicke Streete, or Candlewright streete warde, beginneth at the East end of great Eastcheape, it passeth west through Eastcheape to Candlewright streete. . . . Candlewicke streete tooke that name (as may bee supposed) either of Chandlers, or makers of Candles, both of waxe and tallow."

"On the north side of this warde, at the west end of East cheape, haue yee saint *Clements* lane, a part whereof on both sides is of Candle-wike streete warde, to wit, somewhat North beyond the parish Church of Saint *Clement* in Eastcheape. This is a smal Church, void of monuments."

Wednesday, April 8, 1981

St. Clement, Eastcheap on Clement's Lane is another Wren church built on the foundations of the earlier church. It is unimpressive on the outside, but inside it is plain, square and beautiful. It has a magnificent pulpit but it seemed too much for me to attempt today so I did the seventeenth century white marble font which has the Holy Dove perched within black and gold flames on the wooden cover. What a lovely cooing dove.

The font at St. Clement, Eastcheap

Churchyard of St. Lawrence Pountney

Monday, October 1, 1984

Off early today to do St. Mary Abchurch, but first I came to the churchyard of St. Laurence Pountney, not far from Cannon Street Station. This is the site of a church called St. Laurence Pountney and Corpus Christi College, burnt in the Fire of 1666 and not rebuilt. I found it a few days ago but then it was full of lunchtime visitors. This morning it was quiet, leafgreen shadows and birds singing in the trees made it perfect. A few people passed by in the street below, but other than that I was alone. Both times that I have been there a saucer of milk has been waiting for some favorite cat.

"The parish church of saint *Laurence* was increased with a Chappell of Iesus by *Thomas Cole,* for a maister and Chapleine, the which Chappell and parish Church was made a Colledge of Iesus, and of *Corpus Christi,* for a maister and seuen Chapleins."

72

St. Mary Abchurch

"Then is Abchurch lane, which is on both the sides, almost wholy of this ward, the parish Church there (called of saint *Marie* Abchurch, Apechurch, or Vpchurch as I haue read it) standeth somewhat neere vnto the south ende therof, on a rising ground."

Monday, October 1, 1984
St. Mary Abchurch has the most intriguing churchyard, paved in circles like pinwheels, and there's a medieval crypt beneath it, or so I've read. This Wren church is almost hidden among the buildings around it. It is red brick with a square tower. The inside is, however, surprisingly beautiful. It has a painted dome and clear glass windows. The woodwork is dark and richly carved against the luminous walls above. The lion and unicorn in front of the pulpit seemed to symbolize the fine craftsmanship of Wren's churches. I couldn't resist them.

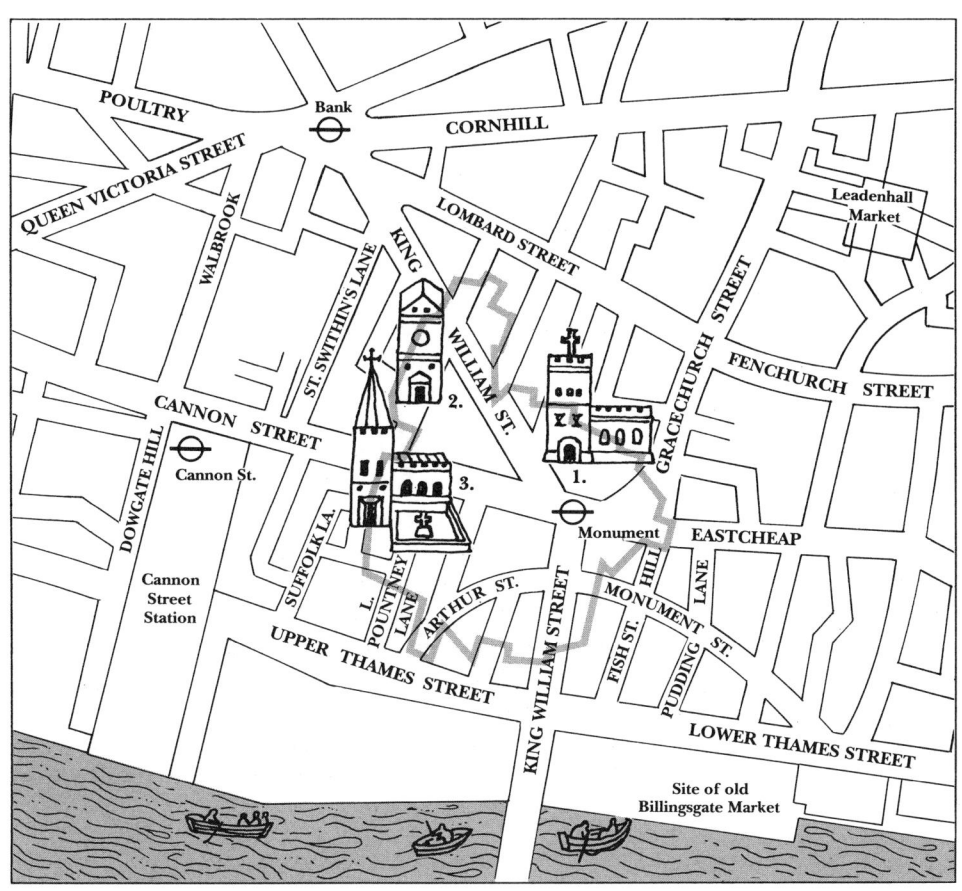

CANDLEWICKE STREET WARDE

1. St. Clement, Eastcheap Church
2. Church of St. Lawrence Pountney
3. St. Mary Abchurch

12.

"Walbrooke warde beginneth at the West end of Candle-wicke streete ward. It runneth downe Candlewicke street west towards Budge row."

Thursday, May 7, 1981

"The said parish Church of S. *Swithen* standeth at the southwest corner of this lane. Licence was procured to new build and encrease the said Church and steeple, in the yeare 1420 Sir *Iohn Hend* Draper, Maior, was an espe-ciall benefactor thereunto, as appeareth by his armes in the Glasse windowes euen in the toppes of them. . . . On the south side of this high streete, neare vnto the channell is pitched vpright a great stone called London stone, fixed in the ground verie deepe, fastned with bars of iron, and otherwise so strongly set, that if Cartes do run against it through neglience, the wheeles be broken, and the stone itselfe vnshaken.

The cause why this stone was there set, the time when, or other memorie hereof, is none, but that the same hath long continued there is manifest, namely since (or rather before) the conquest."

The sun was in and out all day and even a few raindrops fell, but I managed to sketch between showers. On the way to the churchyard of St. Swithen, London Stone, I stopped along Cannon Street to pay my respects to that same stone the church was named for. Today, what is left of this famous stone is set into the facade of the Bank of China opposite Cannon Street Station. This bank is built on the site of John Stow's church of St. Swithen by Lon-don Stone. It was rebuilt after the Fire by Christopher Wren, bombed in 1940, and demolished in 1962. At one time the stone was set into the side of Wren's church. In back of the bank, along Oxford Court, is St. Swithen's churchyard, another lovely spot hidden away among the City's tiny lanes. Today construction was going on all around Oxford Court. Noise and smoke prevailed, so the luncheon crowd avoided the place. All alone there, I was able to get a pretty good sketch. Soon the roses in this garden should be gorgeous.

St. Swithin's churchyard

Mansion House from Royal Exchange courtyard

"Aboute the yeare of Christ 1282 *Henry Wales* Mayor caused diuers houses in this Citty to bee builded towards the maintenance of London bridge: namely one void place neare vnto the parish Church called Woole Church, on the north side thereof, where sometime (the way being very large and broade) had stoode a payre of Stocks, for punishment of offenders, this building tooke name of these Stockes, and was appoynted by him to bee a market place for fish and flesh in the midst of the city."

Saturday, May 9, 1981

I was very bold today. I sat right in front of the Royal Exchange and sketched the passing scene. I focused on Mansion House with Wellington in the foreground. I had to retreat to the massive porch of the Exchange during a rainshower, and that gave me the opportunity to watch two young men working on the huge pots of flowers around that building. London's flowers are a joy. The rain soon stopped and I was able to finish the sketch of this place that has always been the center of the City's busy life. The Stocks Market and St. Mary Woolchurch stood here until the Great Fire destroyed them. They were not rebuilt. Mansion House occupies the site today. Designed by George Dance the Elder, it is the official residence of the Lord Mayor of London.

Monday, April 20, 1981

This is Easter Monday, a Bank Holiday, and only some shivering visitors are left in the City today. I managed a sketch of St. Steven, Walbrook, the church Stow described as being on the banks of the Walbrook. The brook still runs underground, beneath the church today. The sun, at the moment, was shining on a doorway in one of the buildings along Poultry, so I sat there and did a quick sketch of this Wren church. It has one of Wren's most beautiful interiors, built before St. Paul's. It is thought that he experimented with St. Stephen in preparation for the Cathedral. In 1598, in front of the old church, a whipping post was set up to punish vagrant beggars. Today the famous Samaritans, an organization devoted to helping people, have their headquarters here. When I finished my sketch I saw a plaque on the wall of a building near me. It said that St. Mildred, Poultry once stood here. That was another church described by Stow in Cheapeward.

"Downe lower in the streete called Walbrooke, is one other fayre Church of Saint Stephen latelie builded on the east side thereof, for the olde Church stoode on the west side. . . . This church was finished in the yeare 1439 the bredth thereof is sixtie seauen foote, and length 125 foote, the church yearde ninetie foote in length, and thirty seauen in bredth, and more."

"On the banke of the said Walbrooke, at the East end of the high streete, called the Poultrie, on the north side thereof, is the proper Parish Church of S. Mildred, which Church was new builded vpon Walbrooke in the yeare 1457."

St. Stephen, Walbrook

78

Saturday, October 20, 1984

In the afternoon I went to the Dowgate area to see if I
could try sketching the memorial to the church of St.
John the Baptist-upon-Walbrook. It is on Cloak Lane, just
around the corner from the halls of several City
Companies. Consequently, this little street is packed with
cars on weekdays. I've been by many times, but it has
always been too crowded to sketch there. Today there was
more room, and I did a quick drawing of this hidden
memory of John Stow's church. The inscription reads,
"Sacred to the Memory of the Dead interred in the
ancient church and churchyard of St. John the Baptist
Upon Walbrook during four centuries, the formation of
the District Railway having necessitated the destruction of
the greater part of the churchyard. All the human
remains contained therein were carefully collected and
reinterred in a vault beneath this monument A.D. 1884."
That was one hundred years ago.

Memory of St. John the Baptist

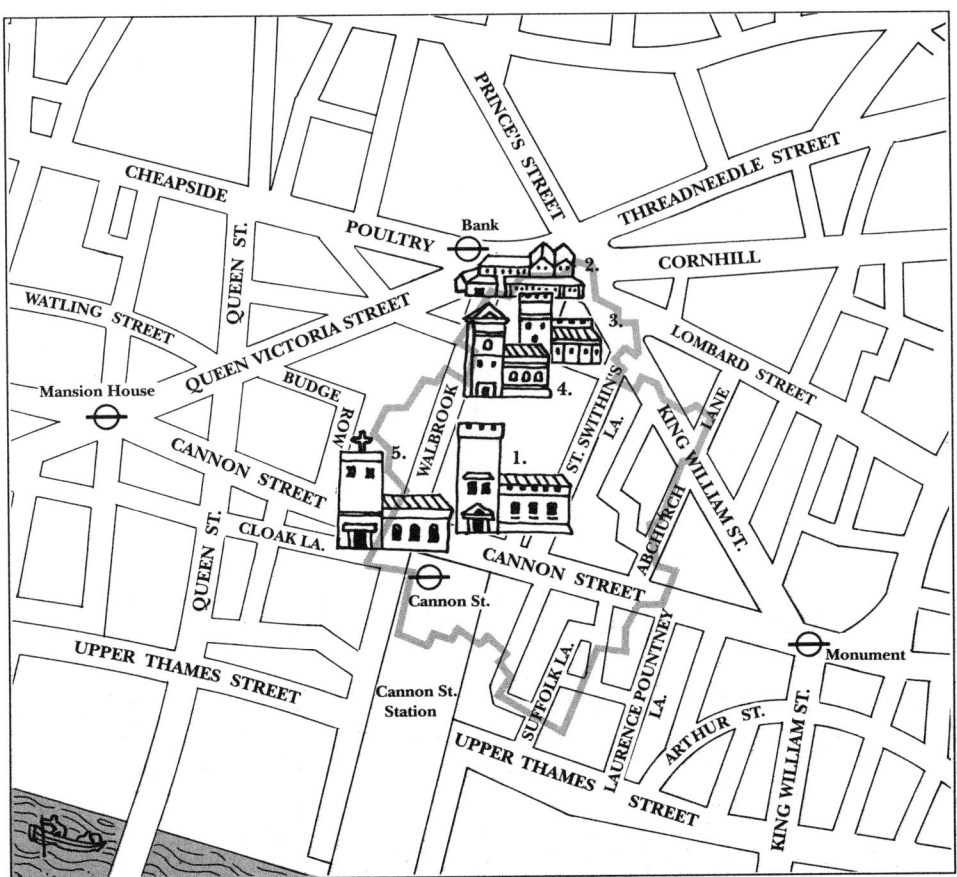

WALBROOKE WARDE

1. Church of St. Swithin, London Stone
2. Stockes Market
3. St. Mary Woolchurch
4. Church of St. Stephen, Walbrook
5. Church of St. John the Baptist-upon-Walbrooke

13.

"Downegate warde beginneth at the south end of Walbrooke warde, ouer against the East Corner of Saint Iohns church vpon Walbrooke, and descendeth on both the sides to Downegate, on the Thames, and is so called of that downe going or descending thereunto: and of this Downegate the ward taketh name."

Thursday, October 11, 1984

The sun was shining when I woke up this morning, and that confused me so much that I took a long time deciding where to go to sketch. I finally ended up at Dowgate Hill. Along this street are a number of City Companies, the Tallowchandlers, the Skinners, the Dyers,

and, around the corner, the Innholders. All except the Dyers were there when John Stow wrote his book.

The Dyers' hall was southeast and nearer to the Thames. Skinners' Hall facade dates to 1790 and is very handsome, but I found it too difficult to sketch along Dowgate Hill. I turned the corner into College Street named for Dick Whittington's College, which was near here. This was Elbow Lane in Stow's time.

I found a quiet place to work under a tree in a little green next to Whittington Square. I sketched the brick arched windows and wall of the Skinners' Hall. I visited this hall in 1981. It's lovely inside, smaller than many of the company halls but with beautiful wood paneling and treasures of ancient wills and deeds and charters. They have been there since 1295. I had almost finished my

Skinners' Hall

"On the west side of this streete is the Tallow Chandlers hall, a proper house, which companie was incorporated in the second yeare of *Edward* the fourth.

Somewhat lower standeth the Skinners hall, a faire house, which was sometime called Copped hall by Downgate. . . .

This companie of Skinners in London were incorporate by *Ed.* the 3 in the first of his raigne. . . . This fraternitie had also once euery yere on *Corpus Christi* day after noone a Procession, passed through the principall streetes of the Citie, wherein was borne more then one hundred Torches of Waxe (costly garnished) burning light, and aboue two hundred Clearkes and Priests in Surplesses and Coapes, singing. . . .

Downe lower haue ye Elbow lane. . . . In this Elbow lane is the Inholders hall, and other faire houses."

drawing when a young man appeared with a lawnmower and, starting at one end of the lawn, he mowed back and forth, coming closer and closer to me. I watched him with a good deal of apprehension. His sullen face told me he had little sympathy for artists. It was a race between my pen and his mower and I finished just in time to retreat before he mowed me down!

Saturday, November 2, 1991
From Trafalgar Square I took a number 15 bus down to the City around Cannon Street. The area was deserted this afternoon as I wandered around familiar places that I had sketched before on past visits. When I came to Dowgate Hill the sun was shining on the intricate iron gate to the Tallow Chandlers' Hall, and that encouraged me to try a drawing from the other side of this lonely street. Ten years ago I had the opportunity to see this livery hall, and I remembered the elegant woodwork of the carved and panelled walls in this very old post-fire hall. Not many people here while I was sketching, workmen mostly, and they seemed rather puzzled to see me there. However a delivery man, hurrying by, added a welcome note of warmth by calling out, "How're you getting along, lov?"

Tallow Chandlers' Hall

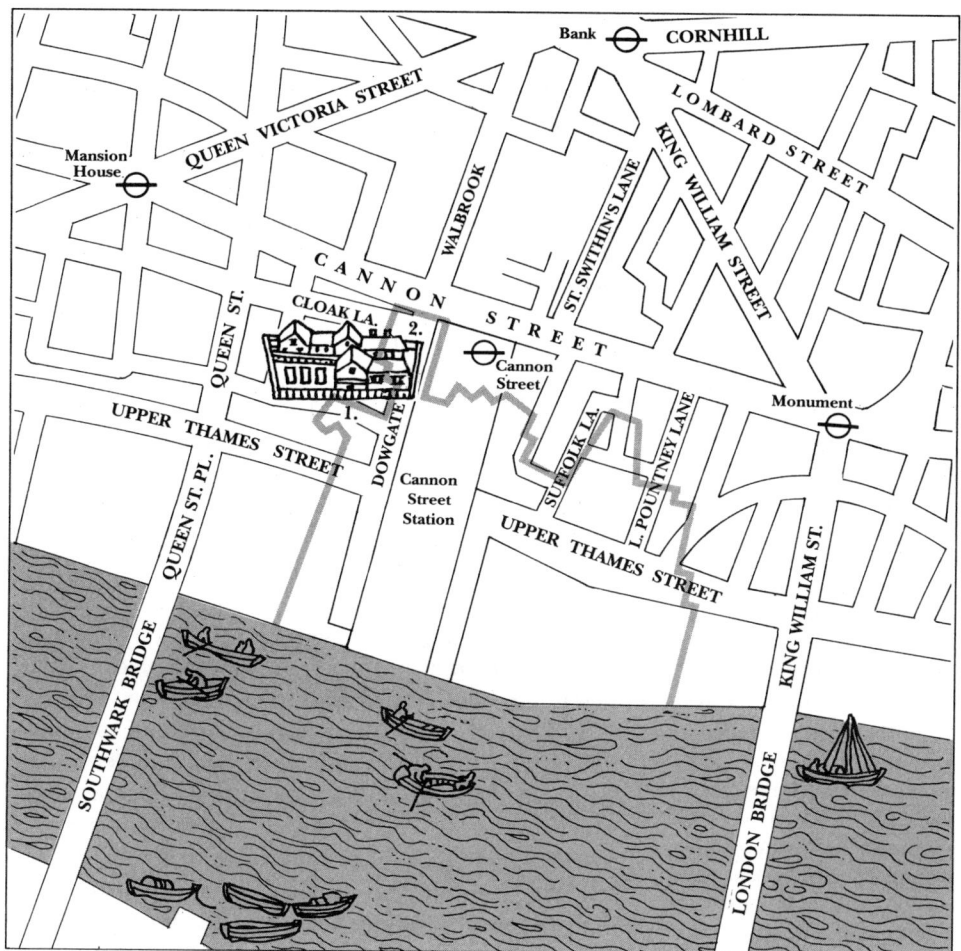

DOWNEGATE WARDE

1. Skinners' Hall
2. Tallow Chandlers' Hall

84

14.

"Now I am to speake of the other wardes, 12 in number, all lying on the west side of the course of Walbrooke: and first of the Vintry warde, so called of Vintners, and of the Vintrie, a parte of the banke of the Riuer of Thames, where the marchants of Burdeaux craned their wines out of Lighters, and other vessels, and there landed and made sale of them."

Thursday, May 7, 1981

"Then is the fayre parish church of S. *Michael* called *Pater noster* church in the Royal, this church was new builded and made a colledge of S. *Spirit*, and S. *Mary*, founded by *Richard Whitington* Mercer, 4 times Mayor . . . this *Richard Whitington* was in this church three times buried, first by his Executors vnder a fayre monument, then in the raigne of *Edward* the 6 the Parson of that church, thinking some great riches (as he said) to bee buried with him, caused his monument to bee broken, his body to be spoyled of his Leaden sheet, and againe the second time to bee buried: and in the raigne of Queene *Mary,* the parishioners were forced to take him vp, to lap him in lead, as afore, to bury him the thirde time, and to place his monument, or the like, ouer him again, which remayneth and so hee resteth."

Another warm day. How pleasant. I left early to do St. Michael, Paternoster Royal. This church is closely tied to one of London's greatest citizens, Dick Whittington. I found the church surrounded by memories of the man. He lived in a house alongside the church and was buried in the church. Actually he was buried there three times according to an intriguing story by John Stow. The lane where he lived is called College Hill. His college was there and two magnificent seventeenth century doors still remain. I would have loved to sketch those doors but the view is impossible, the street is so narrow.

St. Michael, Paternoster Royal was rebuilt to Wren's design after the Fire, and is close by a number of City Company Halls. Its name comes from a nearby street called Paternoster Lane. "Royal" comes from the wine sellers from La Riole near Bordeaux who used to live and sell their wines in this district. The Blitz cleared away many of the buildings between the church and the Thames, and now there is an attractive open space called Whittington Square on the south side of Saint Michael's. I sat there to sketch the base of the tower and a little bit of College Hill.

St. Michael, Paternoster Royal

St. James, Garlickhythe

"Then is the Parish Church of S. *Iames*, called at Garlick hith or Garlicke hiue, for that of old time on the banke of the riuer of Thames, neare to this Church, Garlicke was vsually solde."

Saturday, September 22, 1984

I walked down Garlick Hill this afternoon to sketch the church of St. James, Garlickhythe. I had stopped into this church a few days ago and marveled at its beauty, all clear glass and sparkling light. It has the tallest interior of all Wren's churches. He repaired Saint James after the Great Fire. When it was reopened it cost three and four pence to buy sherry and pipes for the celebration. The church was closed today so I sketched the outside, from Upper Thames Street. I was rather disappointed, I couldn't smell any garlic in the air.

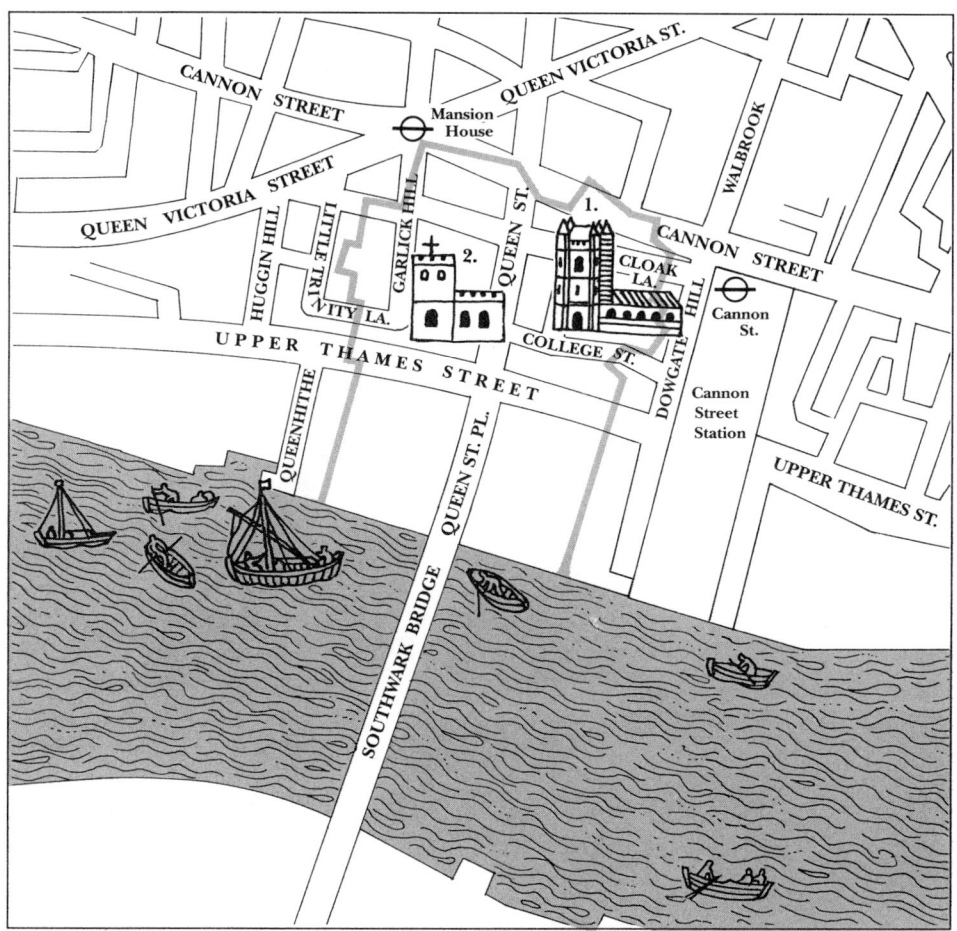

VINTRY WARDE

1. Church of St. Michael, Paternoster Royal
2. Church of St. James, Garlickhythe

St. Mary Aldermary

15.

"The next is Cordwainer streete warde, taking that name of Cordwainers, or Shoemakers, Curriars, and workers of Leather dwelling there."

Saturday, October 6, 1984

"Next . . . is one other fayre Church called Aldemarie Church, because the same was very old, and elder than any Church of saint *Marie* in the Citie, till of late yeares the foundation of a verie faire new Church was laid there by *Henrie Keble* Grocer, Maior, who deceased 1518."

Intermittent sunshine and clouds, and low temperatures today. By sitting out of the wind in a doorway along Queen Victoria Street, I managed to do a watercolor of St. Mary Aldermary, a church first mentioned in 1080. This has a gothic tower, quite unlike Wren's other churches. He was influenced by the earlier tower of Keeble's church and actually used the bottom part of that old tower when he rebuilt St. Mary's after the Great Fire. This is usually a very busy corner, but today the Saturday morning traffic was light and it didn't take long to capture St. Mary Aldermary.

St. Mary-le-Bow

Good Friday, April 12, 1974
A lovely bright blue morning sky for this black robed day
in the church calendar. By afternoon when I sketched St.
Mary-le-Bow, the gathering dark clouds were more suited
to Good Friday. I found a doorway along Cheapside to be

"At the vpper ende of Hosier Lane, towarde West Cheape, is the fayre Parish Church of Saint *Marie* Bow. This church in the reigne of *William Conquerour*, being the first in this Cittie builded on Arches of stone, was therefore called newe *Marie* Church, of Saint *Marie de Arcubus*, or *le Bow* in West Cheaping. . . . The Court of the Arches is kept in this Church, and taketh name of the place, not the place of the Court, but of what antiquitie or continuation that Court hath there continued I cannot learne."

out of the wind and rain as I sketched. This is one of Wren's most impressive steeples. After the Great Fire he rebuilt this church, moving the tower to its present streetside location. He built it on the foundations of an old Roman road. Under St. Mary-le-Bow there are Norman arches, or bows, (it is often called the Bow Church) which form a crypt dating to 1090. The Court of Arches once sat there, now it's at Westminster, (this is where Ecclesiastical Law cases are decided.) The steeple and bells of this church have always been famous. These were the bells that called Dick Whittington back to London, and they are the bells of the old nursery rhyme, "Gay go up and gay go down, to ring the bells of London Town." And of course, only the Londoner born within the sound of the Bow bells is the true cockney. In the last raid of the Blitz in 1941 the bells came crashing down through the tower. Twenty years later they were up again, having been recast at Whitechapel from the old metal. I finished my drawing just as the rains came. The golden dragon atop the steeple was twisting and turning in the swirls of the rainstorm as I left.

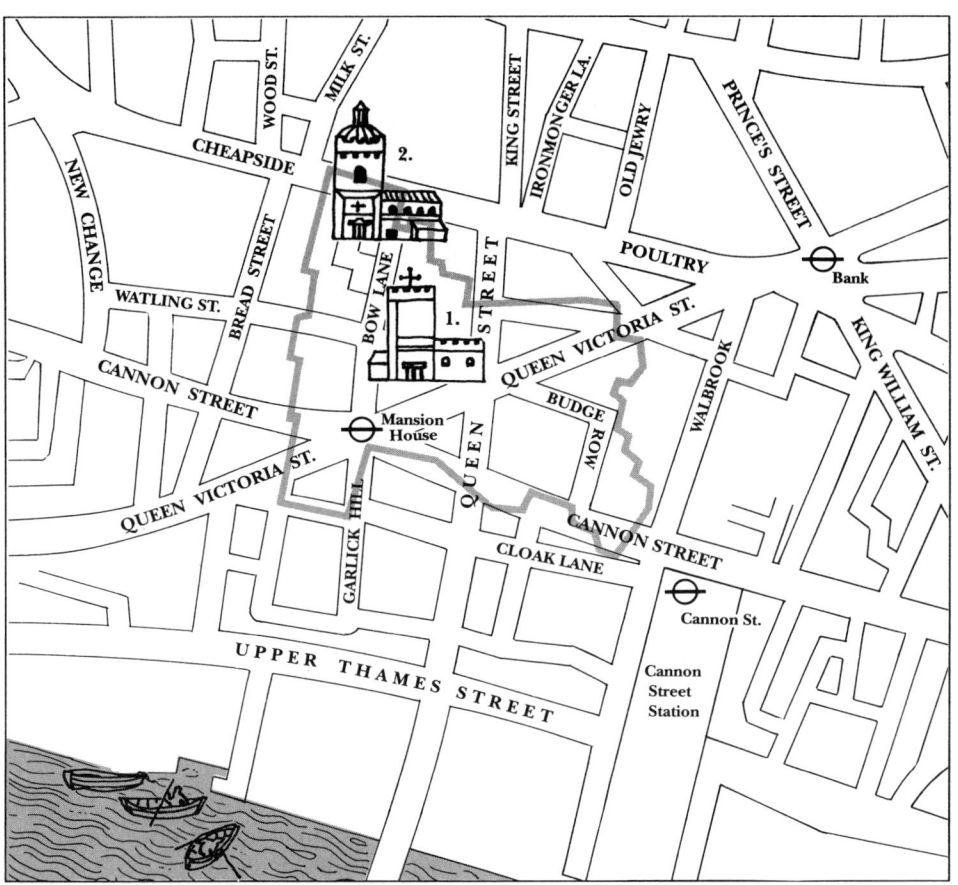

CORDWAINER STREET WARDE

1. St. Mary Aldermary Church
2. St. Mary-le-Bow Church

92

16.

"Next adioyning is Cheape Warde, and taketh name of the Market there kept, called West Cheping."

"This small parrish Church of S. Sith hath also an addition of Bennet shorne, (or Shrog, or Shorehog) for by all these names haue I read it, but the auncientest is Shorne."

"Then in Needelars lane haue yee the parrish church of *Saint Pancrate,* a proper small church. . . . In this Church are buried . . . *Robert Packenton,* Mercer, slayne with a Gunne shot at him in a morning, as hee was going to morrow masse from his house in Chepe."

Saturday, October 6, 1984
In my wanderings today I found the sites of two of John's churches. They are almost side by side along St. Pancras Lane. St. Benet Sherehog and St. Pancras were destroyed in the Great Fire and not rebuilt. Two small open spaces along this dark and cold street mark their places today. This being Saturday, they were closed to the public. I could not get any sort of view from the street. I was disappointed and very grumpy. The feeling lasted until I went to Sadler's Wells in the evening. Three ballets by Ashton restored my good humor.

Saturday, June 6, 1990
This noontime I sat in St. Paul's churchyard and ate a sandwich near the site of Paul's Cross. I gave the last crumbs to the persistently hungry pigeons and walked down Watling Street to Queen Victoria Street and finally found Pancras Lane just off Queen Street. In spite of being here in 1984, I had to really search for it today. I was almost afraid the two tiny churchyards of St Pancras and St. Benet Sherehog might have disappeared. But no, there they were and refreshingly green and well kept. St. Benet's yard was a simple place with low ground cover under a great tree. I sketched the yard of St. Pancras, filled with the leafy movements of tall trees swaying in the breeze and dark shadows and splashes of bright green color. It was lonely and cold there, as in 1984, but I felt grateful that the memory of these two long vanished churches is kept alive in the City today.

Churchyard of St. Pancras

The Guildhall

Thursday, April 20, 1981
A long day in the City today. By 10:30 I was sitting
alongside the church of St. Lawrence Jewry and sketching
the south facade of the Guildhall with its modern red and
white awnings. This facade has been rebuilt and
renovated many times in the past thousand years, but it

"On the North side of this streete is the Guild Hall, wherein the courts for the citty be kept, namely, 1. the court of common counsaile, 2. The court of the Lord Mayor and his Brethren the Aldermen, 3. The court of Hustinges, 4. The court of Orphanes, 5. The two courtes of the Shiriffes, 6. The court of the Wardmote, 7. The court of Hallmote, 8. The court of requestes, commonly called the court of conscience, 9. The chamberlaines court for Prentises, and making them free. . . . The kitchens and other houses of office adioyning to this Guildhall were builded of latter time, to wit, about the yeare 1501."

still bears a remarkable resemblance to the Guildhall that John Stow wrote about. At noon I met John Owen, a friend from home, and we went into St. Lawrence Jewry to the service called the "Spital Sermon." The Lord Mayor and his lady, the Aldermen, and members of the Livery Companies were all there in their colorful gowns. I felt the long continuation of a tradition because John Stow wrote about this same Spital Sermon, and here we were listening to the 1981 version.

After the service we went into the Guildhall to attend the Court of Common Council. We had an intriguing view of the way the City government is carried on. When we left, I went back to finish my sketch of the Guildhall. This time I had many onlookers. As I was finishing, two women stopped to tell me they were cooks in the Guildhall.

"It's a better place to look at than to work in," they complained. I couldn't help wondering how they would have fared if they had worked there in 1501.

The four Civic Virtues

Friday, July 3, 1981
I went to the London Museum today. This is an absolutely fascinating place showing London's past in a dramatic manner. I found the four Civic Virtues, old statues from the facade of the early Guildhall. The inscription read, "The four Civic Virtues 1430. Discipline, Justice, Fortitude, Temperance, trampling a conquered vice in niches in the facade of the Guildhall. Built in 1430, demolished in 1788 and statues sold. Found in a garden in North Wales in 1972." These are the very statues John Stow wrote about. (See Appendix, page 228.) The Museum was crowded with children today, many of them sketching, so I joined them and did drawings of the four enchanting ladies. I got back to the flat in time to make dinner before Bob took me to see "Shoemaker's Holiday" at the Olivier.

It was a perfect show for me.

"Last of all a stately porch entering the great Hall was erected, the front thereof towards the South being beautified with images of stone."

The Great Hall of Guildhall

Tuesday, May 26, 1981

I took refuge in the Guildhall this afternoon when it started to rain. The Great Hall was full of atmosphere and I wanted to try to catch it in a drawing. This time the Hall was empty except for a few visitors wandering about. Their quiet attention and curiosity made me feel that they were as impressed as I was. They were reading the plaques that listed the names of the unfortunate people who have been on trial here: Anne Askew, age 25, a protestant martyr condemned in 1546, and Lady Jane Grey and her husband Lord Guildford Dudley. The one I rather liked was Sir Nicholas Throckmorton. He "was tried in 1554 for High Treason and found not guilty. The verdict was considered unsatisfactory and the jury were sent to prison and only released on paying very heavy fines." That item seemed to relieve the sadness and horror of those plaques. A friendly guard watched the progress of my drawing and assured me, as I left, that he couldn't do as well with a camera.

"This Guilde hall . . . was begunne to bee builded new in the yeare, 1411 the twelfth of *Henry* the fourth, by *Thomas Knoles* then Mayor, and his Brethren the Aldermen, . . . towardes the charges whereof the companies gaue large beneuolences, also offences of men were pardoned for summes of money towardes this worke, extraordinary fees were raysed."

Sunday, June 29, 1981

This is one of the last Sundays before we go home. After some goodbyes at St. Clement Danes, I went down to the City to sketch St. Lawrence Jewry, the official church of the City Corporation. From the outside, St. Lawrence is rather plain and restrained, but inside all is glittering gold and creamy light. I remember the first time I went into this church. I happened to stop by just after a noontime concert. Almost everyone had left. A huge grand piano sat in the aisle before the altar. Someone was turning out the lights and the bright beauty of this church disappeared little by little until only shadows remained. It was very silent. I said a few prayers and left, coming out into brilliant sunshine and a little green garden full of cheerful primroses. I remember sitting there for a few minutes in that sparkling corner of the busy City. Today I went along Gresham Street to find a good view of Saint Lawrence. It's very quiet there on a

"Southwest from this Guildhall is the fayre parrish church of Saint Laurence called in the Iury, because of olde time many Iewes inhabited there about. This church is fayre and large and hath some monumentes."

St. Lawrence Jewry

Sunday afternoon. This was a medieval church before Wren rebuilt it after the Fire, and it was one of the largest and costliest of his churches. It was gutted in the Blitz and later restored. St. Lawrence was the martyr who was roasted to death on a gridiron, and that has become his emblem. The weathervane on the steeple is from the old church, but the shaft is modern, made in the shape of an incendiary bomb.

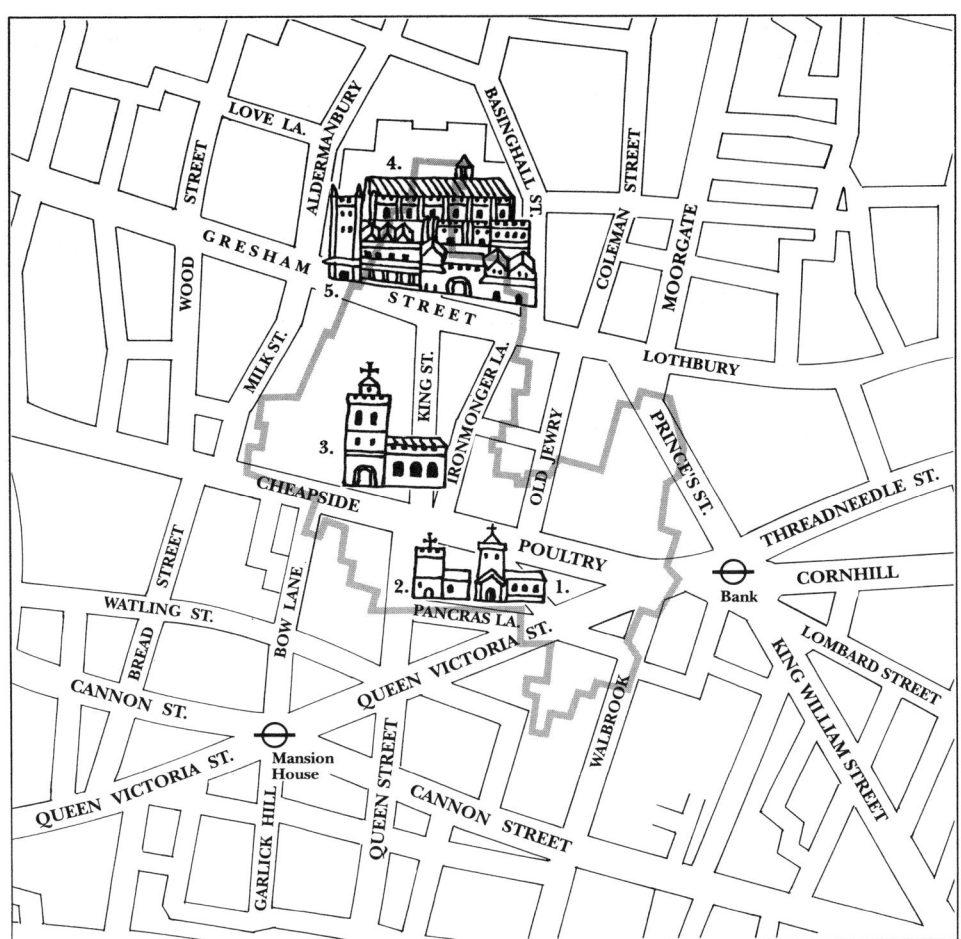

CHEAPE WARDE

1. Church of St. Benet Shrorehog
2. Church of St Pancras
3. Church of St. Mildred, Poultry
   Note: *See page 77.*
4. Guildhall
5. Church of St. Lawrence Jewry

17.

"Next to Chepe Warde on the North side thereof is Colemanstreete Ward, and beginneth also in the East, on the course of Walbrooke in Lothbury and runneth west on the South side to the end of Ironmongers lane, and on the North side to the West corner of Bassinges hall streete."

". . . Ironmonger lane, so called of Ironmongers dwelling there. . . ."

"In this sayde streete, called the olde Iury, is a proper parrish Church of S. Olaue Vpwell, so called in Record, 1320. . . . In this Church, to the commendation of the Parsons and Parishioners, the monumentes of the deade remayne lesse defaced then in many other: first of *William Dikman* Fereno or Ironmonger, one of the Shiriffes of London, 1367. *Roberte Haue-loke* Ironmonger, 1390. . . . *Giles Dewes,* seruant to *Henry* the seuenth, and to *Henry* the eight, Cleark of their Libraries, and schoolemaister for the French tongue to Prince *Arthur,* and to the Lady *Mary* 1535."

Tuesday, March 31, 1981

Went down to Ironmongers Lane today to sketch St. Olave, Jewry. This church was rebuilt by Christopher Wren after the Great Fire. It was demolished in 1888, except for the tower and west front on Ironmongers Lane, and its parish was united with St. Margaret Lothbury. The delightful ship weathervane came from St. Mildred Poultry, which was destroyed only seventeen years before St. Olave. When the site of St. Olave was sold in 1892, a neighbor served notice of easement on the auctioneer because he had been accustomed to step out of his upstairs window to walk and smoke on the roof of the church. Or so I read in my research at the Guildhall Library.

It was lovely there today. A blaze of yellow daffodils in the yard, warm ochres and brown grays in the tower, and the trees just beginning to stir in the early springtime. Two young women came along and stopped to admire my watercolor. They said they worked for an estate business with offices in the church tower and they invited me in to have a cup of coffee, or should I say, "a coffee," as the English do. Inside the tower, the offices were a startling change from the outside. Gracefully modern and light, they are beautifully unique offices for this business concern. Another example of the old and new existing comfortably together.

St. Olave, Jewry

"Now for the North side of this Lothburie, beginning again at the East end thereof, vppon the water course of Walbrooke haue yee a proper Parrish Church, called saint *Margaret,* which seemeth to bee newly reedified and builded aboute the yeare 1440."

Saturday, March 28, 1981

A beautiful sunny and clear day. No buses running, but the tube got me down to Bank station about noon. Very quiet in the City today. From the corner of a building at the intersection of four streets, Gresham, Prince's Street, Lothbury, and Moorgate, I sketched Wren's white Portland stone church of St. Margaret Lothbury in the midst of the Bank area. St. Margaret's is filled with treasures from churches that have disappeared. Starting with the fire of 1666 and ending with the Blitz fires of 1940, many parishes have been united with St. Margaret's. Its parish has this impressive name: St. Margaret Lothbury and St. Stephen, Coleman Street with St. Christopher-le-Stocks, St. Bartholomew-by-the-Exchange, St. Olave, Old Jewry, St. Martin Pomeroy, St. Mildred Poultry, St. Mary Colechurch.

St. Margaret Lothbury

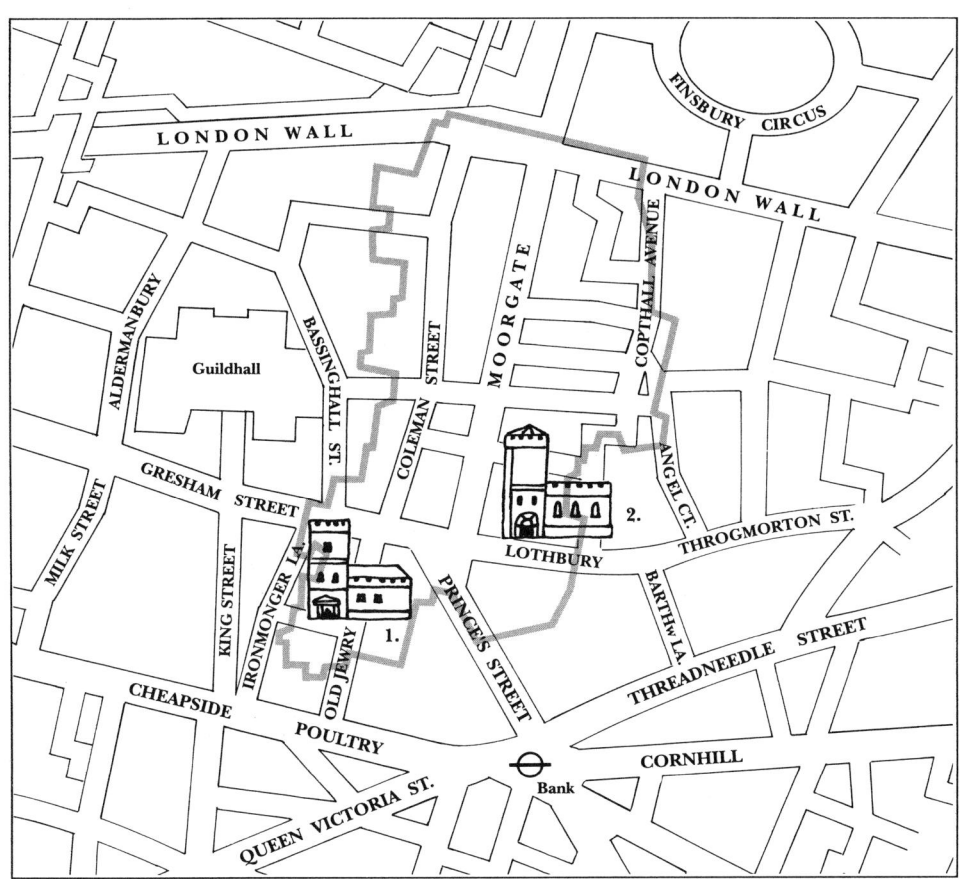

COLEMAN STREET WARDE

1. Church of St. Olave, Jewry
2. Church of St. Margaret, Lothbury

Girdlers' Hall

18.

"The next adioyning to Colemanstreete ward on the west side thereof is Bassings hall warde, a small thing, and consisteth of one streete called Bassings hall streete, of Bassings hall, the most principall house, wherof the ward taketh name."

Tuesday, September 18, 1984

Went back to Guildhall today, to the neighborhood just north of it around Coleman Street. This area was rich in Company Halls when John Stow roamed the City. I was attracted to the Armourers' Hall on Coleman Street and started to look for a good view. Suddenly I saw Girdlers' Hall, and I knew that was to be my sketch. I think that nowhere in the City is the contrast between the modern and the traditional so marked as it is at the north end of Bassinghall Street. Just around the corner on Bassinghall Avenue is Girdlers' Hall on its original site. This elegant early eighteenth-century style brick building was built in 1960 after the previous one was destroyed in the Blitz. It is the third Girdlers' Hall to stand on this site. It looks assured and enduring, and even superior against the backdrop of the soaring construction of London Towers. Of the three Company Halls that John wrote about in this ward, only the Girdlers' remains here today.

"Monuments on the East side thereof, amongst diuerse fayre houses for Marchants, haue ye three halles of Companies, namely, the Masons hall for the first, . . . The next is the weauers hal."

"Lower downe is the Girdlers hall, and this is all touching the East side of this ward."

Site of Coopers' Hall and
St. Michael at Bassishaw

"Next beyond this house be placed diuerse faire houses for marchants and others, till yee came to the backe Gate of Guild hall, which gate and part of the building within the same, is of this warde. Some small distance beyond this gate, the Coopers haue their common hall. Then is the Parish Church of S. *Michaell* called S. *Michaell* at Bassings hall, a proper Church lately reedifyed, or new builded."

Tuesday, May 5, 1981

I sketched along Bassinghall Street this afternoon. I did the steps leading to the wide square at the north end of Guildhall. This is an interesting open space, all stone with a modern green glass fountain and sculpture, trees, shrubbery, and plenty of benches for weary visitors. Quite beautiful in an austere sort of way. I sketched the steps because this is where Coopers' Hall and the church of St. Michael Bassishaw used to be. The church was demolished in 1899, and Coopers' Hall was lost in the Blitz. Two stones in the wall with names and dates remind one of their former role in this Guildhall neighborhood.

While I was sketching a familiar figure came over to chat with me. It was Marisa, a friendly woman I kept meeting as I sketched around this area. She was studying to be a guide for Italian visitors in London. I first met her at the memorial service for John Stow at St. Andrew Undershaft. As we parted I wished her good luck with her exams, and she said, "I'm sure your book on John Stow will be published, do not be discouraged. It will take a few years!" I was pleased at her encouragement. Let's hope she's right.

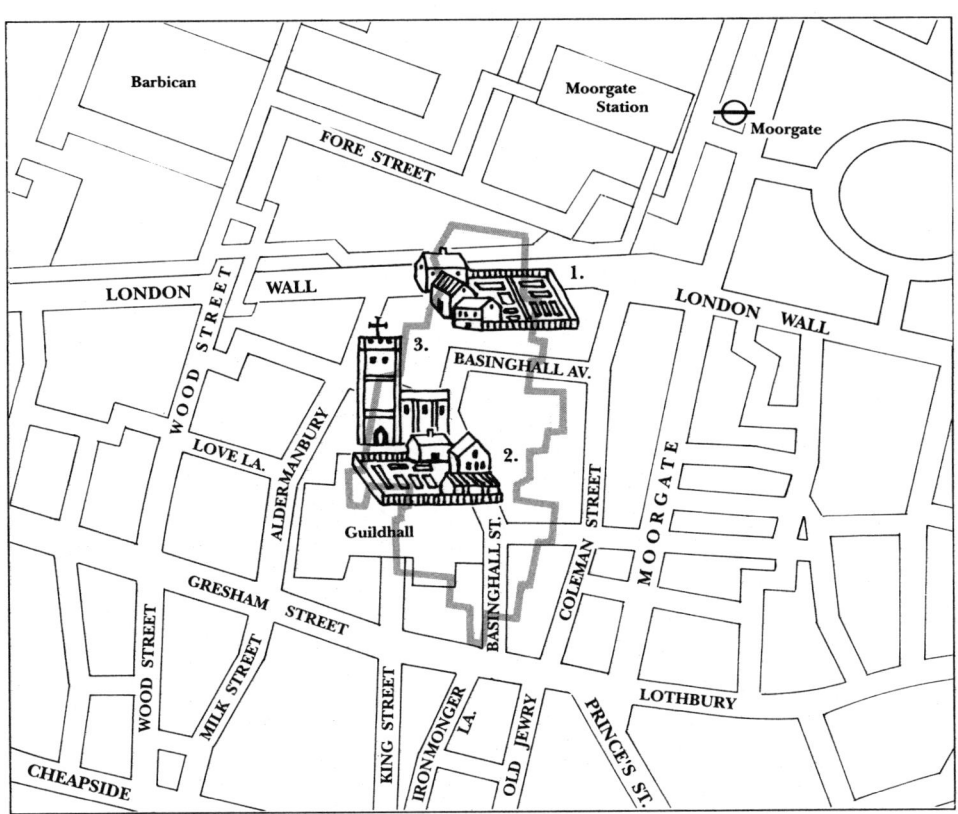

BASSINGS HALL WARDE

1. Girdlers' Hall
2. Coopers' Hall
3. Church of St. Michael at Bassishaw

19.

"The next Warde is called of Cripplesgate, and consisteth of diuerse streetes and lanes, lying as well without the Gate and Wall of the Cittie, as within."

"Then is the parrish church of S. *Mary* Aldermanbury a fayre Church with a church-yeard, and cloyster adioyning, in the which cloyster is hanged and fastned a shanke bone of a man (as is said) very great and larger by three inches and a halfe then that which hangeth in S. *Lawrence* church in the Iury."

Thursday, April 9, 1981

I first saw the open space of St. Mary Aldermanbury in 1974 when a friendly Londoner, wearing a purple shirt, took me there to see a monument to John Heminge and Henry Condell, actor friends of Shakespeare, and editors of the 1623 First Folio. They are buried here. It is a lovely place to sit and relax after working at the nearby Guild-hall library. Today was sunny and warm, and people and pigeons were enjoying the place. Foundations of the old church still remain. I painted the corner with the tablet that tells the story of St. Mary Aldermanbury, "First mentioned in 1181, destroyed by the Great Fire in 1666, rebuilt by Wren, destroyed by bombing in 1940, the remaining fabric moved to Westminster College, Fulton, Missouri, U.S.A., 1966 and restored as a memorial to Sir Winston Churchill."

St. Mary Aldermanbury

Elsing Spital Tower

Monday, May 11, 1981

There are remains of an ancient tower in the Barbican. Every time I looked at it, I wondered how to sketch it. It's hard to see from ground level, so today I just sat on the upper walkway in front of the railing and did what I saw, railing and all. I attracted a few curious onlookers, including an Indian gentleman who has chatted with me before when I have been sketching around here.

This is a fourteenth century tower, first belonging to the small Augustinian Hospital of Elsing Spital, and later to the church of St. Alphage. It was uncovered here after the bombing during the Blitz. Devastated in 1940, this area is now a most exciting part of the City. Old and new combine here in dramatic ways. It's one of my favorite places to walk.

" . . . *William Elsing* Mercer in the yeare of Christ, 1329 the 3 of *Edward* the 3 began . . . the foundation of an Hospitall, for sustentation of 100 blind men, towards the erection whereof, he gaue his two houses in the parishes of S. *Alphage,* and our blessed Lady in Aldermanbury neare Cripplegate. This house was after called a Priorie or Hospital of S. *Mary* the Virgin, founded in the yeare 1332 by *W. Elsing* for Canons regular: the which *W.* became the first Prior there."

St. Alban's Tower, Wood Street

"Then next is Woodstreete....
On the East side of this street
is one of the Prison houses,
pertayning to the Shiriffes of
London, and is called the
Compter in Woodstreet. . . .
Beneath this Compter is Lad
lane . . . and beneath that is
Loue lane, so called of wan-
tons. By this lane is the
parish church of S. *Albon.*"

"The Posterne of *Cripplegate,*
so called long before the
Conquest. . . . so called of
Criples begging there: at
which gate, (it was said) the
body entering, miracles were
wrought, as some of the Lame
to goe vpright, praysing God."

Tuesday, May 12, 1981

Still sketching in this area today, I did St. Alban's tower in
Wood Street. I sat right on the sidewalk along Gresham
Street. People had to walk around me and I was well
aware of some annoyed glances. However this gave a
good view of the church tower with a background of the
Barbican and site of the ancient gate called Cripplegate.
The church of St. Alban was lost in 1666 and rebuilt by
Christopher Wren. Gutted in 1940, only the tower
remains today. One passerby stopped to tell me he was a
freeman of the City and asked if he could buy my
drawing to present it to his Company, the Stockbrokers. I
told him it was destined for another purpose. He seemed
disappointed, but very gentlemanly as he kissed my hand
and said goodby. What a nice way to end my day.

Thursday, October 4, 1984

Yesterday I went to the Salters' Hall open house. Their original hall was on Bread Street. This new and very modern hall is on Fore Street. Their silver collection contains a charming parcelgilt salt made for Elizabeth I in 1580. The salters have a beautiful sunken garden at the base of the ancient wall in Cripplegate. Today I went back to that area and found the remains of the churchyard of St. Alphage, on the opposite side of the wall. This small fragment of churchyard garden is all that remains of the old church. My sketch shows Salters' Hall in the background. St. Alphage was abandoned during the Reformation and its parish moved across the street, taking over the church of Elsing Priory. Right near here was the gate called Cripplegate. The area is rich in Roman remains found after the bombing in 1940 and now restored by the City.

"On the same side is Salters hall, with six almes houses in number, builded for poore decayed brethren of that company: This Hall was burned in the year 1539, and againe reedified."

". . . a parish Church of S. *Alphage,* and the parish Church which stoode neare vnto the Wall of the Cittie by Cripplesgate was pulled downe, the plot thereof made a Carpenters yearde, with saw pittes."

Churchyard garden of St. Alphage

Brewers' Hall

"Not far from thence is the Brewers Hall, a fayre house, which companie of Brewers was incorporated by King *H.* the 6 in the 16 of his raign, confirmed by the name of S. *Mary* and S. *Thomas* the Martyr, the 19 of *E* the 4."

Tuesday, April 7, 1981

I worked in the Guildhall Library during the lunch hour today, the streets being too crowded to sketch at this time. Later in the afternoon I walked down Alderman-bury to London Wall and did a drawing of Brewers' Hall. The Brewers are one of the oldest livery companies. Their charter from Henry VI called ale the "authenticall drink of England." Their original hall, built before 1420, was lost in the Great Fire. The next one lasted until 1940, and the present one was built in 1960 on part of the original site.

It was gray and cool when I started sketching. The pigeons gathered around me looking for leftover lunch. I disappointed them so they nestled among some bright green leaves and contented themselves with small red berries growing there.

St. Giles, Cripplegate

Friday, August 13, 1976

Two years ago Bob showed me "a most interesting place," as he called it, and it surely was. It was the Barbican. Under construction then, it's still under ongoing construction today. I loved it, it was so very exciting and wonderful. This area was almost wiped out during the Blitz. Now a modern community of many levels is growing here, high rise office towers, horizontal streams

116

"Now without the Posterne of Criplesgate, first is the parish Church of saint *Giles* a very fayre and large church lately repaired after that the same was burned, in the yeare 1545 the 37 of *Henry* the eight, by which mischance the monuments of the dead in this church are very fewe."

of flats, houses, shops, pubs, schools, tennis courts, and soon there will be theatres and a museum. Oh, would I ever like to live here! Walkways circle around many levels. In the center of all this is St. Giles Cripplesgate, a church that escaped the fire of 1666 but not the bombs of 1940. The walls and tower remained standing, but the inside was gutted and now has been restored.

These walls and the tower are part of the original church, rebuilt many times. The early church was built in 1090 by Alfune (who also was associated with the building of St. Bartholomew.) He dedicated it to St. Giles, patron saint of cripples and blacksmiths. It stood just outside the City wall in a place that was a bog at the time. In the fourteenth century the area was drained, more people came there to live, and the church was repaired. In 1545 it was rebuilt again after a disastrous fire. Milton and Frobisher were buried in this church, and Oliver Cromwell was married here.

Last time I was here I stood on a walkway high above to watch the London Symphony move into the church for a recording session. Today I found a view from the same walkway looking down on the London wall and moat beside St. Giles. There were few people in the great stone plaza that used to be the churchyard. In the moat were goldfish, huge ones, and deep red pond lilies and tall grasses where little birds flitted about. While I was sketching, two young bobbies came up and asked what I was doing and why. I explained satisfactorily, I guess, for they stayed a while to chat and watch my drawing grow. One of them pointed out a large carp making v-shaped ripples as he swam along the moat. I like to be alone when I'm drawing so I was rather glad when they left. Besides, one of them had a strong accent making it hard to understand him, and of course he was the one who did most of the talking.

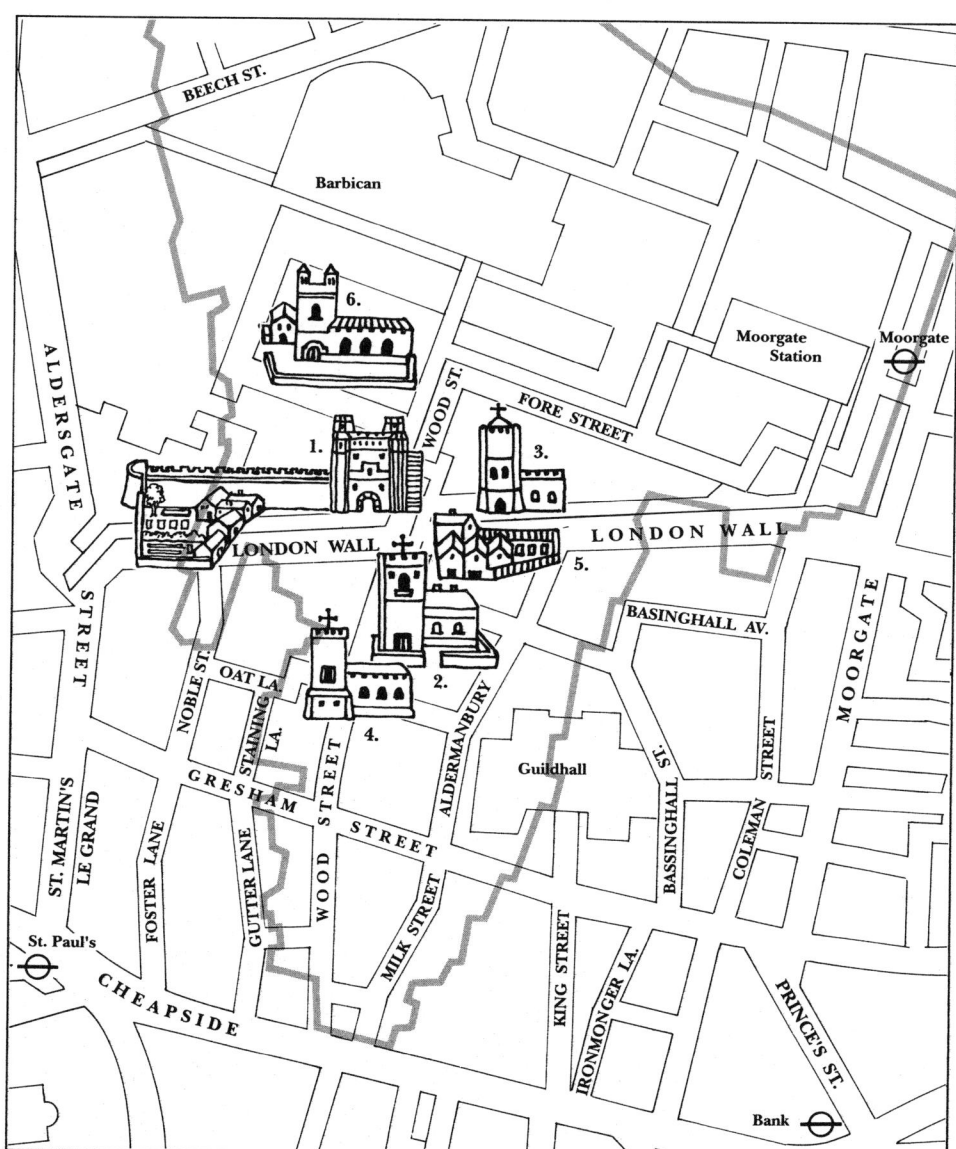

CREPLESGATE WARDE

1. Cripplegate
2. Church of St. Mary Aldermanbury
3. Tower of Elsing Spital and parish church of St. Alphage
4. Church of St. Alban, Wood Street
5. Brewers' Hall
6. Church of St. Giles, Cripplesgate

20.

"The next is Aldersgate Ward, taking name of that north gate of the citie, this ward also consisteth of diuers streetes and lanes, lying aswell within the gate and wall, as without."

Sunday, June 11, 1976

After church I strolled down Giltspur Street. Very quiet this Sunday afternoon. I stopped to do a sketch or two and visit one of my favorite churches, St Bartholomew. When I came out I turned left onto Little Britain and found a perfect view of St. Paul's at the end of this historic street. I stopped right there and started a drawing. I soon realized this was the entrance to a nurse's residence, but friendly smiles and hellos and ohs and ahs at my watercolor made for a very pleasant hour. English nurses have a perky charm all their own.

"And on this west side of Aldersgate streete, by S. Buttolphes church is Briton street, which runneth west to a pumpe, and then north to the gate, which entreth the churchyeard sometime pertaining to the Priory of S. Bartholomew, on the east side."

St. Paul's, from Little Britain

St. Mary Staining churchyard

Tuesday, September 18, 1984

Today I found the churchyard garden of St. Mary Staining. This is one more tiny open space where people come to lunch and relax in pleasant weather. I imagine one of the bonuses of working in the City may well be a green place like this where one can sit surrounded by the freshness of green grass and flowers and bird songs. St. Mary Staining was one of the churches lost in the Great Fire and not rebuilt. The churchyard remains, helping to make life more enjoyable for people around here.

"Then is the small Parrish Church of S. *Mary* called Staining, because it standeth at the North ende of Stayning lane. In the which church being but newly builded, there remayne no monument worth the noting."

"The antiquities be these, first in Stayning lane, of old time so called, as may be supposed, of Painter stainers dwelling there."

120

"Down lower in Wood-streete is Siluer street, (I thinke of siluer smithes dwelling there) in which bee diuers fayre houses. . . .

Then at the North end of Noble streete, is the parrish church of S. Olaue in Siluer streete, a small thing, and without any noteworthy monuments."

Tuesday, April 7, 1981
St. Olave, Silver Street has disappeared but I found its churchyard today. At the corner of London Wall and Noble Street is a little patch of green in front of a modern office building. From a place across the street called London Wall, I did a drawing of all that remains of this old church. St. Paul's hovered in the background in an almost protective manner, or so it seemed to me. John Stow's mention of St. Olave was very brief, but I felt strangely drawn to its exquisite tiny churchyard. It had a curiously touching small stone with an inscription almost worn away, "This is the Parish Church of St. Olave, Silver Street. Destroyed by the Dreadevll Fire in the Year 1666," and below was carved a skull and crossed bones.

Churchyard of St. Olave, Silver Street

St. Anne and St. Agnes

Monday, July 6, 1981

Bright sunshine this afternoon sent me down to Gresham Street to once again try that elusive church of St. Anne and St. Agnes. It needs bright light and shadows, and I think I caught it just right today. Across the street I found a good place to sit in the shade of a great tree in the churchyard of St. John Zachary. These two neighboring churches were lost in the Great Fire, and this churchyard marks the place where St. John once stood. St. Anne and St. Agnes is the church John knew as St. Anne in the Willows. It was rebuilt by Wren after the Fire, badly damaged in the Blitz, and restored in 1966. There's a story told about a vergeress whose determination kept the church open after the war despite strong pressures to close it. Last March I stopped in here to listen to a noontime concert of English Baroque Cantatas. I'm so impressed by the concerts in City churches. Today as I sketched St. Anne and St. Agnes surrounded by a bower of leafy trees, I thought of John's church with the tall ash trees in the churchyard.

"Then is Engaine lane, or Mayden lane, and at the Northwest corner thereof, the parrish Church of S. *Iohn Sachary:* A fayre church with the monuments wel preserued. "

"The parrish church of saint *Anne* in the willowes, so called I know not vpon what occasion: but some say, of willowes growing thereabouts: but now there is no such voyde place for willowes to grow, more then the Churchyeard, wherein do grow some high Ashe trees."

St. Botolph, Aldersgate

Tuesday, May 12, 1981
I've sketched St. Botolph, Aldersgate twice before, but I think today's drawing is the best one I've done. The sun was flashing in and out of the great trees with their black trunks snaking upward through the spring green of Postman's Park. St. Botolph was in dark shadows except for its quaint wooden bellcote catching the sun. The

"In Briten street, which tooke that name of the Dukes of Briton lodging there, is one proper parish church of S. Buttolph. . . . There lie buried . . . The Lady *Anne Packinton* widow, late wife to *Io Packinton* knight, Chirographer of the court of the common pleas: shee founded Almes house neare vnto the white Fryers church in Fleetstreet, the Clothworkers in London haue ouersight thereof."

church is pretty grim on the outside. However, the eighteenth century interior is a delightful surprise. Dark, rich wood panelling, galleries on three sides, and semicircular windows above with light coming in like a waterfall on the rosettes and embellishments below. It is absolutely beautiful, and the monument to Dame Anne Packington is still there! I have paid my respects to Dame Anne, but she is always in shadow and too dark to sketch whenever I've been there.

St. Botolph is another of the medieval churches dedicated to the patron saint of travelers, for it was close by the old City gate called Aldersgate. It's tower was rebuilt in 1627 and was topped by a wooden bellcote. This church escaped the fires of 1666 but had to be rebuilt in the eighteenth century.

Postman's Park was opened in 1887 (the General Post Office is across the street). It was made up of the churchyards of St. Botolph, St. Leonard Foster Lane, and the graveyard of Christ Church Newgate Street. It has a pool where huge goldfish live, and even in February I have seen them there. At lunchtime the park is often filled with lively schoolchildren who've been visiting the Museum of London, which is just across the street.

I was particularily impressed with the cloister in the park. It's called "Heroic Self Sacrifice," and there are many names inscribed of those who lost their lives trying to save others. They are not well known names, just those of mothers and fathers and children and postmen and policemen and firemen and shopkeepers and ordinary passersby. To read these names is a moving experience.

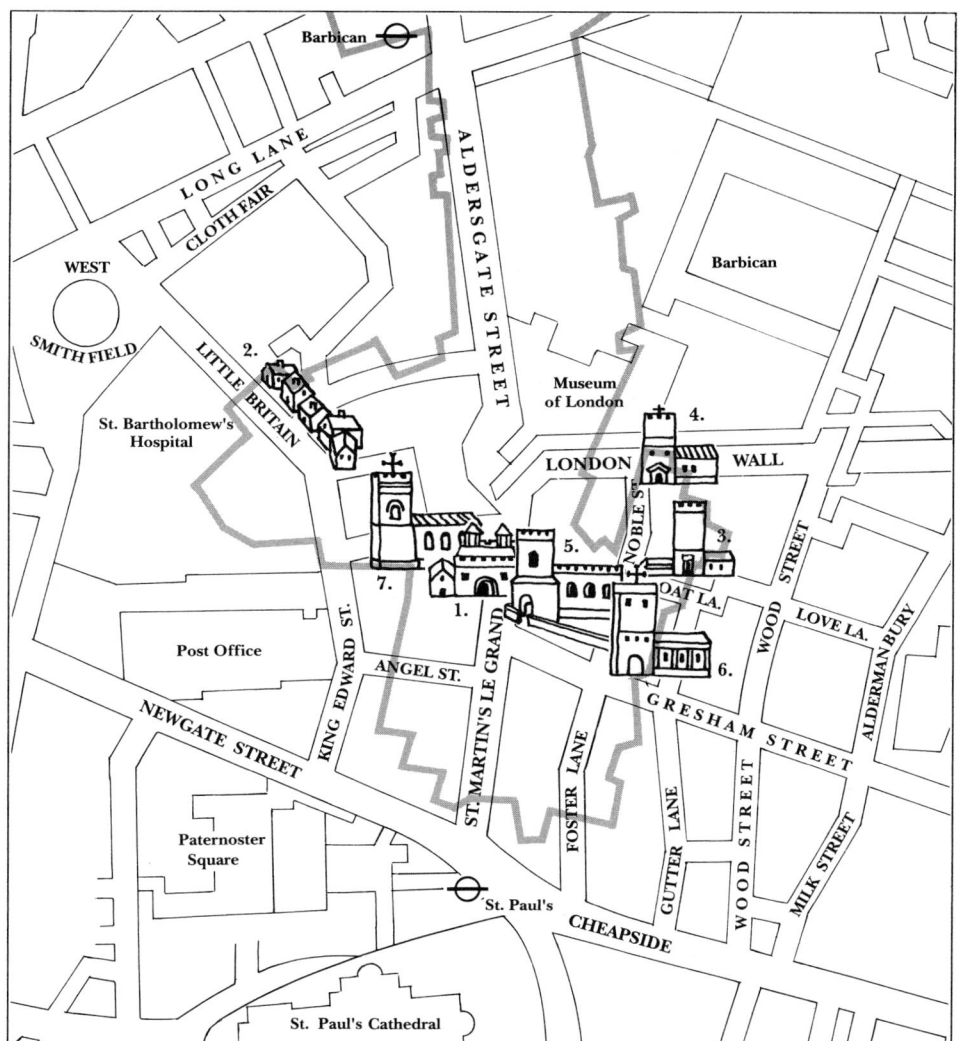

ALDERSGATE WARDE

1. Aldersgate
2. Little Britain (houses)
3. Church of St. Mary Staining
4. Church of St. Olave, Silver Street
5. St. Anne and St. Agnes Church
6. St. John Zachary Church
7. Church of St. Botolph, Aldersgate

Site of the Great Cross at Cheap
and church of St. Peter, Cheap

21.

"On the south side of Aldersgate warde lyeth Faringdon ward, called **infra** *or within, for a difference from an other ward of that name, which lyeth without the wals of the citie, and is therefore called* **Farindon extra**. *These two wardes of old time were but one."*

Tuesday, May 5, 1981
According to Elizabethan maps, the Great Cross at Cheap was about where Wood Street joins Cheapside. John Stow described it as being at the eastern end of Farringdon

Ward within. Wood Street is one of the City's oldest streets, leading to the site of the early Roman fort. Also on Wood Street is a tiny space marking the churchyard of St. Peter Westcheap which was not rebuilt after the Fire. Today I sat along Cheapside and sketched this historic corner. I was lucky to get in a view of St. Peter's churchyard with its famous old plane tree. This corner was one of the City's busiest places in Stow's time, and today it was crowded too. I had a hard time sketching with all the traffic going by. As I worked I thought more and more of that ancient king and queen, and of the stone crosses that Edward erected to his beloved Queen Eleanor (a Victorian restoration of one of these crosses is in front of Charing Cross Station). I was feeling romantically sad as I sketched until a group of small schoolboys stopped to watch me and one of them, shouting in a high shrill voice, "that's fantastic!" jolted me back to the present.

Saturday, June 20, 1990
This has been a splendid day. I worked at the Museum of London this morning during the rainstorm and ended up sketching St. Pancras churchyard this afternoon when the sun broke through the cloudy skies.

In the museum I found a panel of Purbeck marble that was part of Eleanor's Cross at Cheapside. It has the coat of arms of England and, for Eleanor, the coat of arms of the Spanish kingdom of Castile where she was born. She was the daughter of Ferdinand the third. This was truly a love story in Purbeck marble.

"This ward of Faringdon within the walles, is bounded thus: Beginning in the East, at the great Crosse in west Cheape, from whence it runneth West."

"Then next is the great Crosse in west Cheape, which crosse was there erected in the yeare 1290 by *Ed.* the first, vpon occasion thus: Queene *Elianor* his wife died at Hardeby . . . , her bodie was brought from thence to Westminster, & the king in memorie of her, caused in euery place where her body rested in the way, a stately crosse of stone to be erected with the Queenes Image and armes vpon it, as at Grantham, Woborne, Northampton, stony Stratford, Dunstable, S. Albones, Waltham, west Cheape, and at Charing, from whence she was conueyed to Westminster, and there buried."

"At the Southwest corner of Woodstreet, is the parish church of S. *Peter* the Apostle, by the said Crosse, a proper Church lately new builded."

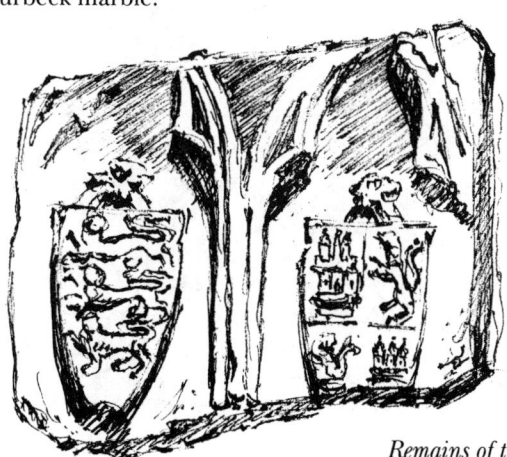

*Remains of the cheap Cross
at the Museum of London*

Tower of Christ Church

Saturday, June 2, 1990

I sketched Christ Church tower in 1984, but at the time it was half hidden by scaffolding. I went down Newgate Street this morning to try it again. The tower is all that remains today of Christopher Wren's great church after the Blitz devastated this area north of St. Paul's.

Greyfriars Monastery, a powerful religious order, once stood here. Its huge church was second only to Paul's and was the burial place of four queens, according to John Stow. The Greyfriars had their own private entrance in the City wall. Christ's Hospital, the famous Bluecoat School, was here too. Actually it was here until 1902 when it was moved out of the City. There are many stories told about the children. Unwanted babies were sometimes left at the doors of the church as well as at the school, causing disagreements as to whether the church or the school should be responsible for them. When Wren rebuilt this church after the Fire, he used steeply raked galleries so the children could be in full view all the time. No more chances for them to race about and hide in enclosed galleries!

I sat in the doorway of a restaurant that was closed for alterations and I was continually interrupted by people asking when it would be open, very unhappy they were. I could hear workmen inside and presently the door opened and a man in a white shirt with rolled up sleeves asked me if I would like a cup of coffee. Of course I would, and it was good coffee and a welcome break. Before I left I went inside and showed the work crew my drawing. They were pleased and I was even more pleased to realize I was in an old American landmark, a Burger King!

"Then the late dissolued Church of the Gray Friers: the originall whereof was this.

The first of this order of Friers in England, nine in number, arriued at Douer: fiue of them remained at Canterburie, the other 4 came to London . . . they hyred an house in Cornhill of *Iohn Trauers,* one of the shiriffes of London. They builded there litle cels wherein they inhabited, but shortly after . . . the number of the Fryers so increased, that they were by the Citizens remoued to a place in S. *Nicholas* shambles. . . .

Margaret Queene, second wife to *Edward* the first, began the quire of their new church, in the yere 1306. . . .

In the yeare 1552 began the reparing of the Gray Fryers house, for the poore fatherlesse children. And in the month of Nouember, the children were taken into the same to the number of almost foure hundreth. On Christmas day in the afternoone, while the Lord Mayor and Aldermen rode to Powles, the children of Christs Hospitall stood, from saint *Lawrence* lane end in Cheape, towards Powles, all in one liuery of russet cotten, 340 in number. And at Easter next, they were in blew at the spittle, and so have continued euer since."

130

"Then is the North church-yard of Powles, in the which standeth the Cathedrall church, first founded by *Ethelbart* King of Kent, about the yeare of Christ, 610. . . .

The first of February, in the yere 1444 about two of the clock in the afternoone, the steeple of Powles was fired by lightning. . . . This steeple was repayred in the yeare 1462 and the Weather-Cocke agayne erected: *Robert Godwin* winding it vp, the rope brake, and hee was destroyed on the Pinacles, and the Cocke was sore brused."

Tuesday, May 7, 1974
Another blue sky day, not so cold as yesterday. Wandering around St. Paul's area I came upon a spectacular view of the cathedral from the great wide stairs called Peters Hill. I crossed Victoria Street and found a place to sit close by the Salvation Army Headquarters and did a drawing of this historic spot. The church called St. Benet, Paul's Wharf was on my left and the seventeenth century College of Arms was across the street. I felt as though I was sitting in the middle of London's history.

St. Paul's Cathedral from Peter's Hill

132

Friday, September 21, 1984

Spent most of the day around St. Paul's. First I went to
the Information Centre on the south side of Paul's to
pick up a ticket for the October third open house at
Salters' Hall. Then I walked down Sermon Lane to
Knightrider Street and its little square. Such romantic
names! However Sermon Lane has nothing to do with
sermons, and Knightrider Street has all but vanished in
today's City. I sat in the square and did a quick sketch of
St. Paul's immense dome swirling above the tiny street.
To be so close looking up at this magnificent building is
like looking at infinite beauty created by one man,
Christopher Wren. Well, the old cathedral was no less
wonderful, according to John Stow.

St. Paul's from Knightrider Court

St. Paul's churchyard and
St. Augustine's tower

Wednesday, August 4, 1976
I sketched the east end of St. Paul's churchyard this afternoon, catching a bit of Paul's and the tower of St. Augustine-with-St. Faith. Just beyond used to be St. Paul's school, founded by Dr. John Colet, a friend of Erasmus. Rebuilt a number of times, the school was moved out of the City in 1884. Today there is a new school beside the tower, the Choir School of St. Paul's.

St. Augustine's black steeple with its tall slender onion is a reconstruction of Wren's steeple which was damaged in the Blitz. It was lead covered, now it is fiber glass. It is still a beautiful shape, cutting into the blue sky like a delicate silhouette.

"The parish church of S. *Augustine* . . . This is a fayre church, and lately well repaired."

"At the West ende . . . vnder the Quire of Paules, also was a parrish Church of Saint Faith, commonly called S. Faith vnder Pauls, which serued for the Stacioners and others dwelling in Paules Churchyard."

"In the east parte of this Churchyeard, standeth Powles schoole, lately new builded and endowed in the yeare 1512 by *Iohn Collet* Doctor of Diuinity, and Deane of Powles, for 153 poore mens children to be taught free in the same schoole."

St. Vedast, Foster Lane
and site of Paul's Cross

"And then Fauster lane (so called of Saint *Fausters*, a fayre Church, lately new builded)."

"About the middest of this Churchyeard is a Pulpit Crosse of timber, mounted vpon steppes of stone, and couered with leade, in which are sermons preached by learned Diuines euery Sundaye in the forenoone. The very antiquity of which Crosse is to mee vnknowne."

Thursday, March 12, 1981
After weeks of reading in the Guildhall Library, it was great to be out sketching again. I wanted to do St. Vedast, Foster Lane, so I strolled through St. Paul's churchyard looking for a good view. I found it, and something else too. At my feet was a circular design carved into the pavement with the words, "Here stood Paul's Cross." What more could I ask for? The site of Paul's Cross and St. Vedast in one sketch! Stow knew this church as St. Fauster. Its name has slowly changed through the years to St. Vedast. When Wren rebuilt the old church after the Fire he built on the medieval foundations. The southeast corner wall is the original one.

Friday, August 7, 1987

At last the great sprawling construction across from Christ Church is now finished, and it turns out to be the Telecom Building. Somehow it makes Wren's tower stand out even more in all its exquisite beauty. The morning light filtered into the little garden at the base of the tower and I sat there a few minutes and thought about John Stow's description of this place. The early church had a library started by Dick Whittington in 1429, which had "twentie eight desks, and eight double setles of Wainsco."

I had one more sketch to do today so I continued on to St. Paul's to visit the crypt once more, hoping to find something I'd missed before. Well, I did find something and I could hardly believe my eyes. The tomb of Nicholas Bacon is still there! He was Lord Keeper of the Great Seal at Elizabeth's court, and one of her close friends for many years of her long reign. He had survived the Great Fire of 1666, but he'd lost his arms and legs. Yet even with his scarred face, he looked noble and stately. Time has not dimmed his charm and authority.

"Sir *Nicholas Bacon,* Lord Keeper of the great Seale, on the South side of the Quire, 1578."

Nicholas Bacon at St. Paul's

"In this street on the north side, is the Parish church of saint *Martin,* a proper church, and lately new builded: for in the yeare 1437 *Iohn Michael* Maior and the comminaltie, granted to *William Downe* parson of S. *Martins* at Ludgate, a parcell of ground, conteyning in length 24 foot, and in breadth 24 foot, to set and build theyr steeple vpon, &c."

Wednesday, April 10, 1974

A gray morning brightened up with hot cross buns for breakfast. I left the flat about ten thirty and went down to Ludgate Circus to look for another nursery rhyme church I'd read about in the Guildhall Library. St. Martin-within-Ludgate is on Ludgate Hill just below St. Paul's. According to the booklet I bought in the church, the old St Martin's was close by Ludgate, one of the great gates to the City. The church burned in the Great Fire and was rebuilt by Wren on its early foundations. Its slender dark spire was planned by Wren to be a foil for St. Paul's magnificent dome. The guidebook said that the Middlesex Yeomanry trumpeters play a fanfare from the balcony of the spire on May Day. I'd love to hear that!

While I was reading the booklet, the verger and vicar came over to talk. They seemed very enthusiastic about an American artist wanting to sketch their church. The vicar suggested I might like the view from the parking lot across the street on Ludgate Hill.

The parking lot was an old bomb crater (I keep being reminded of the war). The place was full of parked cars. I rested my drawing pad on the hood of a car and started sketching. The attendant noticed me and came rushing over to demand to know, in a strident voice, what I thought I was doing there. Then he saw my drawing and all changed. He stayed a while and chatted about how he came to be there. He'd been hired for three months and had been there eleven years. He was formerly a chauffeur to "the bloke who owned the place." I finished my drawing and as I was leaving he called out, "Goodby and good luck, darlin."

St. Martin-within-Ludgate

Blackfriars

"In the yere 1529 Cardinall *Campeius* the Legat, with Cardinal *Woolsey* sate at the said blacke friars, where before thcm as Legats & Iudges, was brought in question the kings marriage with Queene *Katherin* as to be vnlawfull, before whom the king and Queene were cited and summoned to appeare, &c. . . .

The same yeare in the Moneth of October began a Parliament in the Blacke Friers, in which Cardinall *Woolsey* was condemned in the premunire."

Tuesday, March 18, 1981

The streets to the southwest of St. Paul's are a fascinating interlocking of narrow and twisting lanes. This is the area of the great Dominican Priory at Blackfriars. Two open spaces mark the place where it once stood. Today I sketched one of them. Beside a pile of stones a black and gold sign read, "This fragment of wall is all that now survives above ground of the site of the Dominican Priory. It formed part of the south wall of the provincial's hall. In 1965 it was given a stone backing for security." Beside sketching, I did a bit of gardening. I had brought along a little primrose plant that was not doing too well in our flat. I planted it at the base of a tree growing there and hoped it would take a new lease on life in this quiet spot. As I was sketching, a tall, slender young man came hesitantly up the steps to gaze at the pile of stones. He glanced over and smiled. I nodded, "That's all that is left!" so he came over and we had a long chat. We were both so pleased to find someone else who was interested in these ancient places. He was an English student of history.

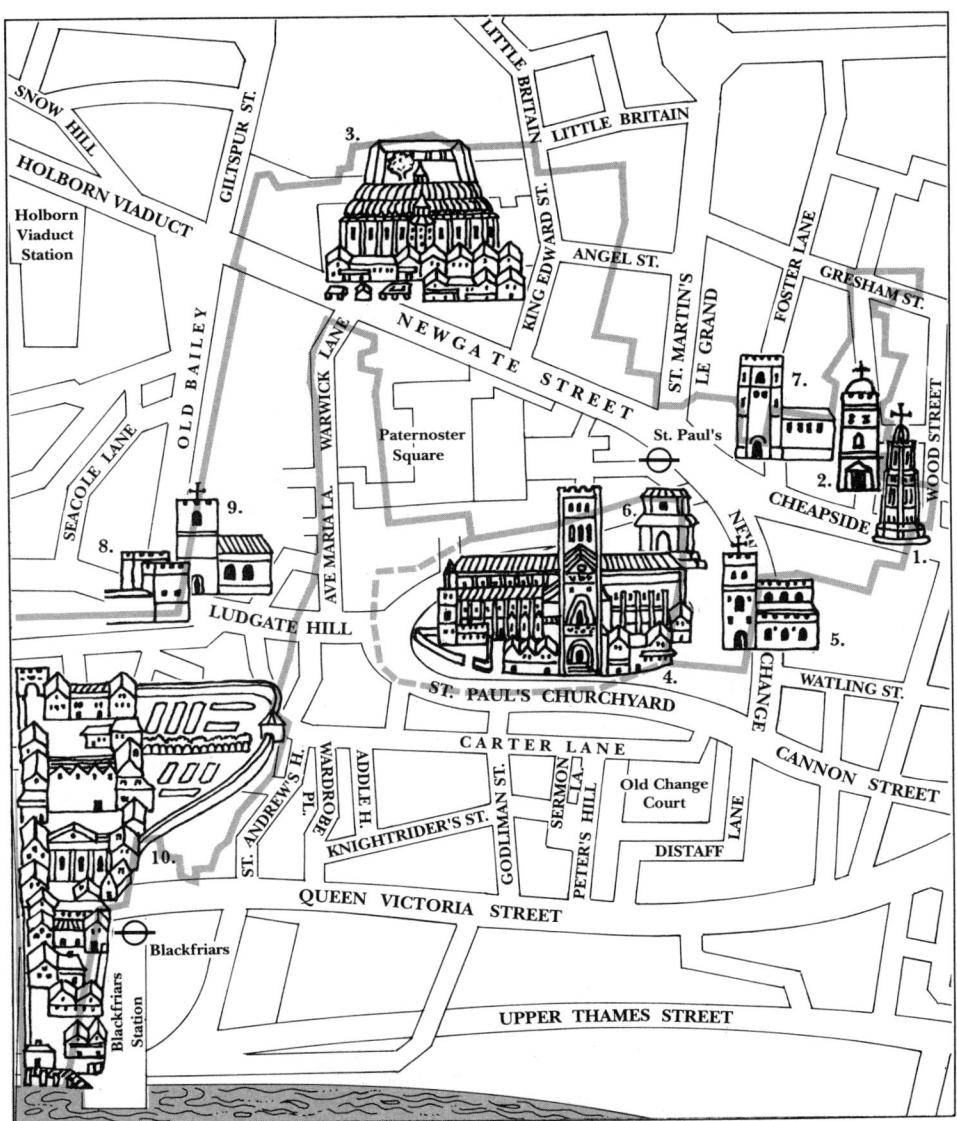

FARINGDON WARD WITHIN

1. Great Cross at Cheap
2. Church of St. Peter, Westcheap
3. Christ Church and Greyfriars Monastery
4. St. Paul's Cathedral
5. Church of St. Augustine-with-St. Faith,

6. Paul's Cross
7. Church of St. Vedast, Foster Lane
8. Ludgate
9. Church of St. Martin-within-Ludgate
10. Dominican Priory at Blackfriars

22.

"Bredstreete Ward beginneth in the high streete of west Cheape, to wit, on the south side, from the Standard to the Great Crosse. . . . Then is Bredstreet it selfe, so called of bread in olde time there sold."

Friday, March 20, 1981

"In this Distar lane, on the north side thereof, is the Cordwayners, or Shoomakers hall. . . . Of these Cordwayners, I reade, that since the fift of *Richard* the 2 (when he tooke to wife *Anne* daughter to *Vesalans* King of Bohem) by her example the English people had vsed piked shooes, tied to their knees with silken laces, or chaynes of siluer and gilt, wherefore in the fourth of *Ed.* the 4 it was ordayned and proclaimed, that beakes of shoone and bootes should not passe the length of two inches, vpon paine of cursing by the Cleargie, and by Parliament to pay xx. s. for euery payre."

After doing a miserable drawing in the morning, I was in a glum mood, and couldn't find anything I wanted to sketch. I finally collapsed onto a bench in St. Paul's Gardens to have lunch and a cup of tea in this most historic place. A plaque on the wall read, "On this site stood six successive Livery Halls of the Cordwainers' Company." The first hall was built in 1440 and the last one demolished in the Blitz. Today the Cordwainers have their hall in Lincoln's Inn. After lunch I revived enough so I could see a sketch right in front of me. Just across the garden the sun was shining on St. Augustine's tower with the shadowy St. Paul's behind it. The twisting trees were still bare, but the grass was brilliant green. Such dramatic color, the Cathedral was dark umber and ochre and St. Augustine was glistening white. When Bob and I were here in 1976 we met the architect, Bob Crayford, who was working on the cathedral. He restored the doorway in this tower.

St. Augustine's tower from
the site of Cordwainers' Hall

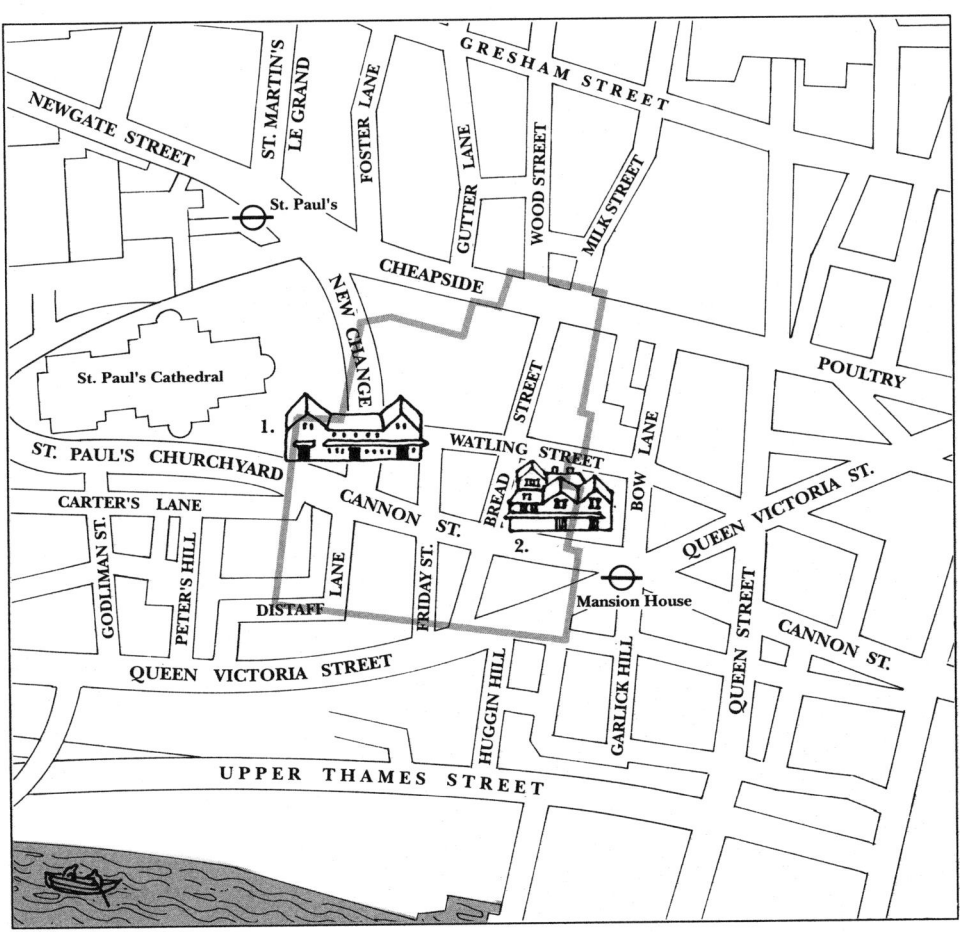

BREDSTREETE WARDE

1. Cordwainers' Hall
2. Salters' Hall

23.

"Next vnto Bredstreete Warde on the south side thereof, is Queene Hithe warde, so called of a water gate, or harborow for boates, lighters, and barges, and was of old time for shippes."

Thursday, March 19, 1981

"Towardes the west end of Knightriders street is the parish church of *S. Nicholas Cold Abbey*, a proper church, somewhat ancient, as appeareth by the wayes raysed thereabout, so that men are forced to descend into the body of the church: it hath bin called of many *Colden Abbey*, of some, *Cold Abbey*, or *Cold Bey*, & so hath the most ancient writings, as standing in a cold place, as Cold harbor, and such like."

The large square on the south side of St. Paul's is called Old Change Court, named for the street John Stow knew as Old Exchange. After lunch I went there to sketch. What a place this is! From the courtyard a panorama of churches lay before me, St. Paul's, St. Augustine, and farthest to the south, St. Nicholas Cole Abbey. St. Nicholas was the first Wren church to be completed after the Great Fire. It was burned out in 1941, but has since been restored. St. Nicholas is on Queen Victoria Street, which is on a level well below Old Change Court. My watercolor shows only the upper part of the church. A very old ship weathervane rides atop the handsome lead spire. In ancient times there was a fish market near here and the fishmongers attended this church, so the weathervane carries on the old association.

St. Nicholas Cole Abbey

Cleary Garden

Wednesday, September 19, 1984

This was a great day for sketching. I left quite early for St. Paul's area and walked southeast, aiming for St. Mary Somerset. I started a drawing there three years ago and left it on the sketching pad. As I walked along Queen Victoria Street I found a delightful place called Cleary Garden. It is very choice, with old brick walls and beautifully landscaped terraces reaching down toward Upper Thames Street. Small signs indicated the brick walls were very old, some pre-fire. Remains of houses that John Stow may have known? He mentioned Huggen Lane and Painters' Hall. Huggen Hill runs along the east side of this garden and Painters' Hall is still here too. This morning the garden was very damp, but I sat down and did some sketching, with wet grass and branches and leaves poking at me. I'm grateful to the City for preserving these bits of old London, unearthed when Queen Victoria Street was built.

From there I walked over to St. Mary Somerset and finished the drawing that rain had interrupted three

"Then is Spuren Lane, or Spooners lane, now called Huggen lane."

"In Trinity lane, on the west side thereof, is the Painter stayners hall, for so of olde time were they called, but now that workemanship of stayning is departed out of vse in England."

144

"The Parrish Church of Saint Mary Summerset, ouer against the Broken Wharfe: it is a proper church, but the monumentes are all defaced."

"Last of all, haue you Lambart hill lane, so called of one Lambart owner thereof."

years ago. Wren rebuilt St. Mary Somerset after the Fire. It stood until 1871. Then it was torn down, the tower alone left standing. The Blitz did some damage, but now it's restored. I sat at the top of Lambeth Hill to do my sketch. Afterwards I walked down the hill to look at the tiny churchyard below.

St. Mary Somerset

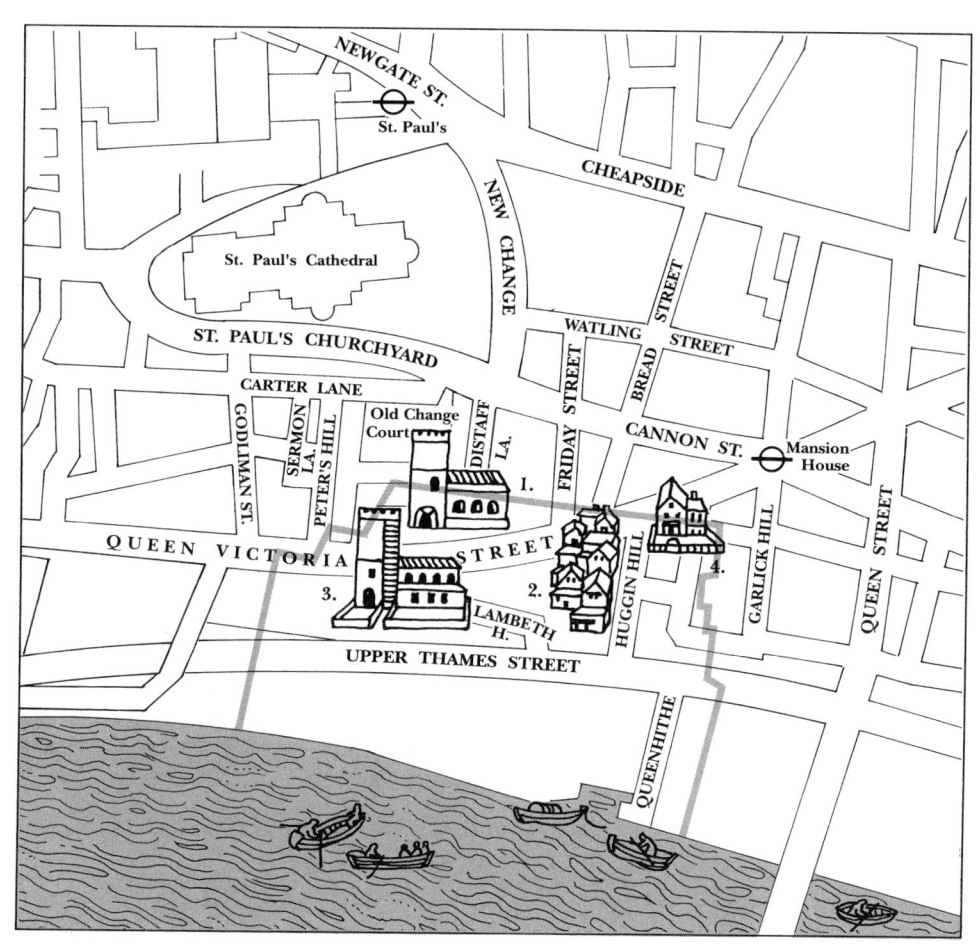

QUEENE HITHE WARDE

1. Church of St. Nicholas, Cole Abbey
2. Houses at Huggin Hill
3. St. Mary Somerset Church
4. Painter Stainers' Hall

St. Benet, Paul's Wharf

24.

"The next is Castle Bainard Warde, so named of an olde Castle there."

Monday, April 13, 1981

A dark, gray, and damp morning. We marketed and did the laundrymat detail, so I didn't leave for St. Paul's area until eleven thirty. I walked over to Peter's Hill and sat on the steps to do a drawing of St. Benet, Paul's Wharf. This is a Wren church, not at all like his other churches. It is absolutely delightful, sort of a red brick cube with swags over the tall, narrow windows. The tower has a fat little round cupola and small spire. It looks as though it should be a church for children, but it is for the Welsh community in London. It is one of the few City churches that stands by itself, not hemmed in by neighboring buildings. Inigo Jones, one of the first great English architects, is buried in St. Benet's. His paternal grandfather was Welsh.

"Touching lanes ascending out of Thames streete, to Knightriders streete, the first is, *Peters* hill, wherein I find no matter of note, more then certaine Almes houses, lately founded on the west side thereof, by *Dauid Smith* Imbroderer, for 6 poore widowes, whereof each to haue 20 s. by the yeare."

"S. *Benet* Hude (or Hithe) ouer against Powles Wharffe, a proper parish Church, which hath the Monuments of Sir *William Cheiny* knight, and *Margaret* his wife, 1442 buried there."

St. Andrew-by-the-Wardrobe

"Then turning vp towardes the North, is the parish church of S. *Andrew* in the wardrobe, a proper church, but few Monuments hath it. *Iohn Parnt* founded a chauntry there."

". . . the first of these Castels banking on the Riuer Thames, was called *Baynards Castell,* of *Baynarde* a noble man that came in with the Conquerour, and then builded it."

Thursday, March 26, 1981

This was a busy day. Bob went with me to the market early this morning and by noon I had preparations for dinner well under way. I decided, on the spur of the moment, to dash down to St. Andrew-by-the-Wardrobe to finish the sketch I started last Saturday. The colors were lovely this afternoon, light reds and browns, soft and warm. Even the nearby pub, called Castle Baynard, was bathed in the same rosy colors. St. Andrew's is a Wren church, well restored after the Blitz. Its tower is plain and handsome with a beguiling weathervane that came from St. Michael Bassingshaw when that church was demolished in 1900. It didn't take long to turn my sketch into a watercolor and I was back home in plenty of time for our little dinner party in the evening with Michael Rose, our landlord.

Friday, September 21, 1984

In 1981, when I was wandering around the area to the south of St. Paul's, I came across Wardrobe Place, site of the King's Wardrobe. Today I had to search a bit before I found it again. It was tucked away in a maze of streets not far from St. Paul's and close by St. Andrew-in-the-Wardrobe. This little lane, with its elegant doorways (some are eighteenth century) and old world atmosphere was a charming surprise. An ornate brick gateway was at the far end. In the garden great pots of flowers and plants spilled onto the paved courtyard, and leafy trees cast dancing shadows on the old stones. The King's great Wardrobe, the house that John Stow wrote about, was destroyed in the fire of 1666.

"Then is the kings greate Wardrobe. . . . In this house of late yeres, is lodged sir *Iohn Fortesque,* knight, Maister of the Wardrobe, Chancellor and vnder Treasurer of the Exchequer, and one of her Maiesties most honourable priuy Councell. The secret letters and writings touching the estate of the Realme, were wont to be enroled in the kings Wardrobe."

Site of the King's Wardrobe

"Then is the Stacioners Hall on the same side, lately builded for them, in place of *Peter* Colledge, where in the yeare, one thousande fiue hundred fortie and nine, the fourth of January, sixe men were slaine by the fall of earth vpon them, digging for a Well."

Monday, August 2, 1976

I wandered around Amen Court and Stationers' Hall Court this afternoon. I can never resist walking a few steps further to see what lies beyond a doorway or gateway. Behind Stationers' Hall I found a small cottage nestled in an enchanting garden. Few people walked through here and those who did seemed startled to see me sketching. One man hurrying by stopped to say, "This was a garden in Tudor times and it is still a garden today." Another was rather brusque as he came up to me, "What are you doing . . ." then he saw the sketch on my lap, and continued "oh, very nice, very nice indeed!" and walked away quickly. When I finished the drawing I sat there for a few moments, all was so still. The sounds of the City were muted and far away. The years sit lightly in this sheltered place.

Stationers' Hall

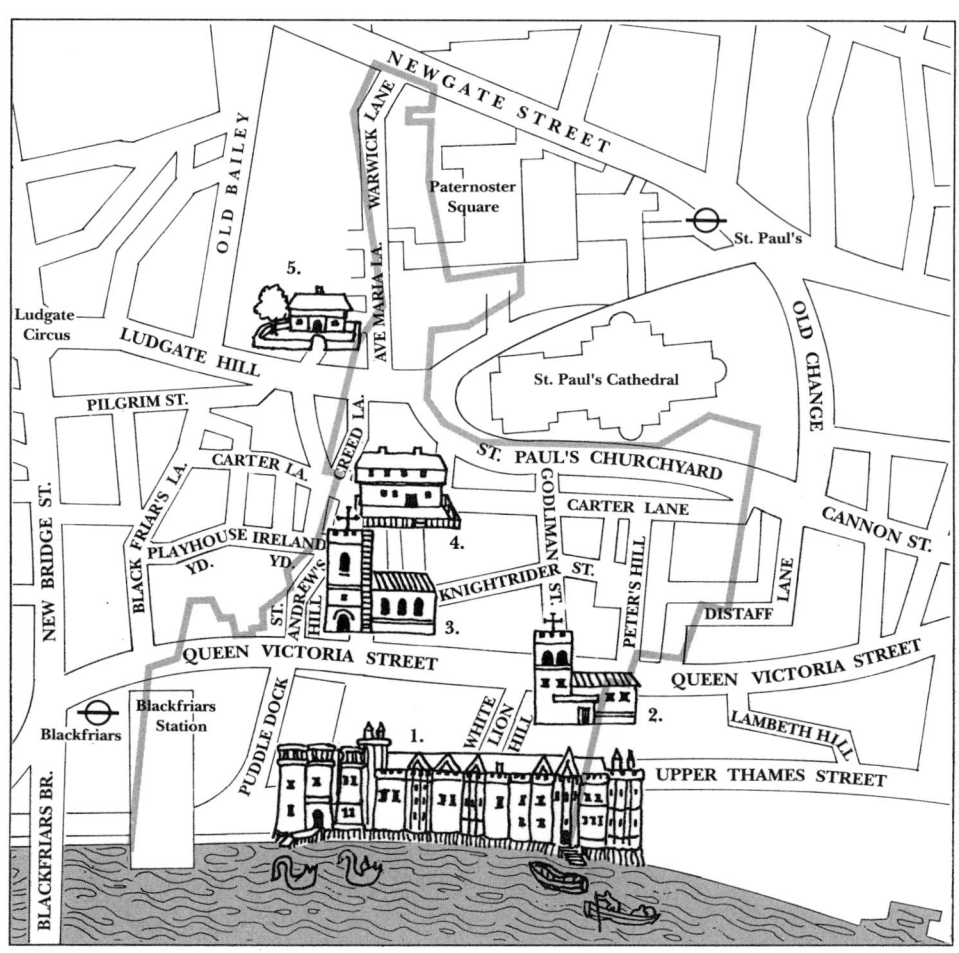

CASTLE BAYNARD WARDE

1. Baynard's Castle
2. Church of St. Benet, Paul's Wharf
3. Church of St. Andrew by-the-Wardrobe
4. The King's Wardrobe
5. Stationers' Hall

25.

The Golden Boy at Pie Corner

"The farthest West Ward of this Cittie, being the 25 Warde of London, but without the Walles, is called Faringdon without, and was of old time part of the other Faringdon within."

". . . a way towardes Smithfield, called Guilt spurre, or Knightriders streete, of the knightes and other riding that way into Smith fielde, replenished with buildings on both sides vp to Pie corner . . . and ouer against the said Pie corner lyeth Cocke lane."

Sunday, July 11, 1976

It was quite hot after church as I walked over to Smithfield via Ludgate Hill, Old Bailey, and Giltspur Street. I stopped to sketch the Golden Boy of Pie Corner. He is a rotund boy, symbol of the "sin of gluttony," and he used to decorate the front of an old tavern called The Fortune of War which was destroyed in the Great Fire of 1666. The Golden Boy was saved and now he stands high on the side wall of a building at the corner of Cock Lane. He reminds all passersby that the dreadful fire ended at this spot after burning 395 acres of London.

Tuesday, February 14, 1974

A day of great contrasts, all a part of London's history woven into today's life. Smithfield Market, the wholesale meat market of London, is in West Smithfield on the site of St. Bartholomew Fair. A cloth fair was first held here in the twelfth century when England was a great exporter of wool and cloth. Rich in history ever since, Smithfield was where young King Richard II saw Wat Tyler slain in the Peasants' Revolt of 1381. This was the place of many tournaments and joustings. Here also martyrs were burned at the stake in the sixteenth century. Today it's an amazing market where London's meat is distributed early every morning. Victorian iron and glass halls, intricate gateways, hundreds of white coated butchers in a frenzy of activity, thousands of pounds of beef, lamb, pork, game, and poultry hanging from myriad hooks or piled high on hand carts being pushed out to the trucks lined up in the arcades, and this was at ten thirty near closing time. I am sure I would not have been able to sketch here had I come earlier. I was able to do a few quick sketches, and the butchers had time to gather around and chat with me, always ending with "How about drawing me, luv?"

"Beyond this Pie corner lyeth west Smithfield, compassed about with buildinges. . . .

And thus much for encroachment . . . of this Smithfield, whereby remaineth but a small portion for the old vses, to wit, for markets of horses and cattle, neither for Military exercises, as Iustings, Turnings, and great triumphes which haue been there performed before the princes and nobility both of this Realme and forraigne countries."

"The 48 of *Edward* the third, Dame *Alice Perrers* (the kings Concubine) as Lady of the Sunne, rode from the Tower of London, through Cheape, accompanied of many Lords and Ladies, euery Lady leading a Lord by his horse bridle, till they came into west Smithfield, and then began a great Iust, which endured seuen days after."

Smithfield Market

154

St. Bartholomew-the-Less

". . . the large hospitall of S. *Bartilmew,* founded by *Rahere* the first Prior of S. *Bartilmewes* thereto neare adioyning, in the yeare 1102.

Alfune . . . became the first Hospitelar, or Proctor for the poore of this house, and went himselfe dayly to the Shambles and other markets, where hee begged the charity of deuout people for their reliefe, promising to the liberall giuers . . . rewarde at the handes of God."

Tuesday, May 5, 1981

A warmer day, full of sunshine and sudden showers. Just the sort of day that lures you into a sketch and then rains on it! But no matter. I went down to Smithfield to sketch the fifteenth-century tower of St. Bartholomew-the-Less. This church is inside the grounds of St. Bartholomew's Hospital. It was built on the site of one of the medieval chapels of the hospital. This is the oldest hospital in London still on its original foundations. Affectionately known as St. Barts, it is famous the world over. I sat by the fountain in the square outside the hospital and started sketching the tower. All went well for a while, until a group of actors arrived on the other side of the fountain. There was a young king of England in a long black coat with a red fox collar, a slender youth with a crown on his head, another in Levi's and tee shirt, a director with a loud voice, a script girl with a weird hairdo, technicians

with mikes and cameras, and a dozen others milling around. This was upsetting, but I didn't want to interrupt my drawing. They paid no attention to me, so I continued working. Then the rain came. The actors were well prepared with large umbrellas, but I had to retreat to the shelter of St. Bartholomew the Great across the square. When the rain stopped I returned to my place at the fountain. The acting company was still there. The rain could not deter them, but something else did. A locked car with a horn that would not stop screaming drove them away. I felt sorry for them, but when I left they were still holding forth at one of the gates to the market. The tradition of acting still invades Smithfield.

"Ye may read in *Anno* 1391 a play by the parish Clearkes of London at the Skinners well beside Smithfield: which continued three dayes togither. . . . Of late time in place of those Stage playes, hath beene vsed Comedies, Tragedies, Enterludes, and Histories, both true and fayned."

*The Lady Chapel of
St. Bartholomew-the-Great*

"... the late dissolued priorie of *S. Bartilmew* founded also by *Rahere*, a pleasant witted Gentleman, and therefore in his time called the kinges Minstrell....

This Priorie at the late surrender, the 30 of *Henrie* the eight, was valued at 653 li. 15 s. by yeare.... The Church being pulled downe to the Quire, the Quire was by the kings order annexed for the enlarging of the olde Parish church ... and so was vsed till the raigne of Queene *Marie,* who gaue the remnant of the priorie church to the Friers preachers, or black Friers, and was vsed as their couentual church vntill the first of our Soueraigne Ladie Queene *Elizabeth,* those Friers were put out, and all the saide church with the old parrish church was wholy ... giuen by parliament to remaine for euer a parrish Church to the inhabitants within the close called great *S. Bartholomewes.*"

Tuesday, July 6, 1976

The heat continued today. Very uncomfortable. Sketching in St. Bartholomew the Great, I did two parts of the Lady Chapel for my series on places in London of special interest for Americans during this bicentennial year. The reason for doing the Lady Chapel is that Benjamin Franklin had a printing press here. It's hard to imagine now, walking through this absolutely magnificent church, but at one time the Lady Chapel was rented out for all sorts of unchurchly business. I found this great Norman priory church rather overwhelming. Its beauty had such a spiritual quality. It was founded in 1123 by Rahere. As the story goes, Rahere was a "frivolous" courtier of Henry I. On a pilgrimage to Rome he fell ill and saw visions of St. Bartholomew the Apostle, who told him to go back to London and build a priory and hospital at Smithfield. He did this, and here is all that remains of his priory church. The present hospital across the square continues on the site of Rahere's hospital.

There were few visitors today, but one of them was a painter who came in wearing white overalls and no shirt. He said, "I'm working nearby and when I saw this church I thought I'd like to have a look." The verger was pleased to tell him the history of the church. When he said Henry VIII had "pinched all the valuables and looted the place," the painter replied, "Well he had a lot of expenses. Cost a lot to keep all those wives." I could see where the painter's sympathies lay. The verger spoke of Henry VIII and Cromwell as though they were present-day enemies of his.

The Lady Chapel

Churchyard of St. Bartholomew

Saturday, April 18, 1981

Saturday before Easter and very cold. I almost decided to forego sketching, but after lunch the sun was shining so I headed for St. Bartholomew's, stopping along the way to pick up a watercolor pad at Winsor & Newton. It was very quiet around Smithfield this holy Saturday, only a few visitors with cameras strolling about.

I wanted to paint the churchyard of St. Bartholomew because John Stow wrote about attending a contest of schoolboys speaking in St. Bartholomew's churchyard. It probably was not this very place, but certainly nearby. I sat on a cushion of newspapers and did a corner of the great church and its tiny yard with yellow daffodils and black gravestones. While I was working, young boys were playing in the garden area below me. Their voices and the choir rehearsing Easter music inside the church were the only signs of life in this ancient place. When I finished I was very cold, and glad to come out into the brilliant sunshine of the square of West Smithfield. I sat in the small park for a while to soak up the warmth and watch a young couple enjoying themselves with a beautiful collie.

"The arguing of the Schoole boyes about the principles of Grammer, hath beene continued euen till our time: for I my selfe in my youth haue yearely seene on the Eve of S. *Bartholomew* the Apostle, the schollers of diuers Grammer schooles repayre vnto the Churchyard of S. *Bartholomew,* the Priorie in Smithfield, where vpon a banke boorded about vnder a tree, some one Scholler hath steppcd vp, and there hath apposed and answered, till he were by some better scholler ouercome and put downe: and then the ouercommer taking the place, did like as the first: and in the end the best apposers and answerers had rewards, which I obserued not but it made both good Schoolemaisters, and also good Schollers, diligently against such times to prepare themselues for the obtayning of this Garland."

St. Sepulchre-without-Ludgate

Wednesday, April 10, 1974

After sketching St. Martin-within-Ludgate, I walked along the street called Old Bailey, coming out at the Criminal Courts Building. Diagonally across the street is St. Sepulchre-without-Newgate, one of the churches in my nursery rhyme. I went into the church and found it fascinating, much of London's turbulent past is gathered in this place. The porch and tower were built in 1450, the organ has its original casing of 1670, and the piscina bears traces of the Great Fire. I could go on and on. And then there is the Execution Bell, a sad little bell with a haunting history. It was rung outside the cells of condemned prisoners at midnight to announce the day had come when they were to prepare themselves for the trip to the gallows at Tyburn. Very grim. I stopped to sketch an intricately carved Christopher Wren font cover before going outside to do a drawing of the tower. This is the tower with a peal of ten bells mentioned in the nursery rhyme, "When will you pay me? Say the bells at Old Bailey." I sat across the street, slightly sheltered by Holborn Station, and settled in a corner to sketch Saint Sepulchre with the traffic of Holborn Viaduct rushing and whirling around it.

"Now to returne through Giltspurre streete by Newgate, where I first began, there standeth the fayre parish church called Saint *Sepulchers* in the Bayly, or by Chamberlaine gate, in a fayre Church yarde, though not so large as of old time, for the same is letten out for buildings, and a garden plot."

Font cover by Wren

Old Bailey

Thursday, June 9, 1981

Morning came in damp and drizzly. By noon it looked better and I headed down to the City to sketch the Ccntral Criminal Courts Building, rather affectionately known as "Old Bailey." This is where Newgate Prison once stood. Newgate was one of the medieval city gates, and it also housed a jail. I found a good view from the churchyard of St. Sepulchre, but had barely got out my sketch pad when it became misty and wet again. Went into the church for a bit. There were only two or three others there, sitting quietly in deep meditation (or sleep.) The old verger came along and announced everyone must leave. He whispered confidentially to me that he had to "get them out!" Very odd, I thought. It was really raining now. I took shelter across the street under the overhang of Holborn Station and used the time to sketch the police station just down Snow Hill. This station had a blue plaque saying it was on the site of Saracen's Head Inn. When I finished, the sun was shining. I went back to the churchyard and did a drawing of Old Bailey with Justice reigning over all, sword in one hand, scales in the other.

"The next gate on the West, and by North, is termed *Newgate*, as latelier builded then the rest, and is the fift principall gate. . . . This gate hath of long time beene a Gaile, or prison for fellons and trespassers, as appeareth by Records in the raigne of king *Iohn.*"

"Now on the left hand or south side from Newgate, lieth a street called the Old Bayly, or court of the Chamberlaine of this citty."

"Next to this Church is a fayre and large Inne for receipt of trauellers, and hath to signe the Sarasens head."

Saracen's Head Inn

Tuesday, September 25, 1984

St. Etheldreda's Church is pure magic. What a chapel the Bishop of Ely had! I was captivated by this ancient church. Built around 1300 (its crypt is even older), this is the only remaining part of the London residence of the Bishop of Ely. On its old walls were modern sculptures of people who had worshipped there and died for their faith. I tried a sketch of two of them, John Houghton, a Carthusian prior who was hanged at Tyburn in 1535, and "Anne Line, Sempstress," who was caught aiding a priest. She also was hanged at Tyburn. Preparations for Mass in this Catholic church were beginning, so I went outside and did a watercolor of the ancient door to the crypt. A steady stream of communicants passed along the upper entrance to the chapel. How poignant it must be to worship here and feel so close to those early martyrs.

"Then is the Bishop of Elies Inne, so called of belonging and pertayning to the Bishops of Elye. . . .

Thomas Arundell Bishoppe of Elie, beautifully builded of new his Pallace at Elie, and likewise his Mannors in diuers places. . . . In this house for the large and commodious roomes thereof, diuers great and solemne feastes haue beene kept."

St. Etheldreda's Church

St. Andrew, Holborn

"On the other side at the very corner standeth the parish church of *S. Andrew*, in the which church, or neare there-vnto was sometime kept a Grammer schoole. . . . There bee monuments in this church of . . . *Raph Rokeby* of Lincolnes Inne Esquier, Maister of saint Katherines. . . . He gaue by his Testament to Christes Hospitall in London 100 li., to the colledge of the poore of Queene *Elizabeth* in east Greenwich, 100 pound, to the poore scollers in Cambridge, 100 pound, to the poore schollers in Oxford 100 pound."

Thursday, February 15, 1974
Did a quick sketch today of the base of the tower at St. Andrew, Holborn. This tower is fifteenth century. I was intrigued by the quaint figures of two Charity Children, a boy and girl, that were over the door. I stood in a small garden area to sketch them. They came from a nearby parochial school and have a special reason for being here. Captain Thomas Coram is buried in this church. He was the great benefactor of abandoned children who built the Foundling Hospital in 1739. On one of our recent walks, Bob pointed out Coram's Fields playground and the famous hospital for sick children in Great Ormond Street. Coram's work continues today.

Thursday, May 21, 1981

I left this morning to find the statue of Queen Elizabeth. I found her high above a school door in St. Dunstan-in-the-West, a church on Fleet Street. Originally she graced the City gate called Lud Gate. John Stow mentioned a "picture" of the Queen and I think he was writing about this statue. I copied the inscription, "This Statue of Queen Elizabeth formerly flood on the Weft fide of LUDGATE That gate being taken down in 1760 to open the Street was given by the CITY to SR FRANCIS GOSLING, KNt ALDERMAN of this WARD who caufed it to be placed here."

I finished my drawing as raindrops began to fall, so I stepped into St. Dunstan's. A Rumanian orthodox communion service was going on in one part of this octagonally shaped church. Incense, candles, rich color, ornaments and monuments on the walls (some from the sixteenth century) made this a warm and exciting interior. I was glad the rain had chased me indoors.

"From this Conduit vp to Fewtars lane and further, is the parish church of S. Dunstan, called in the west, (for difference from S. Dunstone in the east.)"

"In the West is the next, and sixt principal gate, and is called *Ludgate*. . . . The 28 of Queene *Elizabeth* . . . the same yere the whole gate was newly and beautifully builded, with the Images of *Lud,* and others, as afore, on the East side, and the picture of her Maiestie, Queene *Elizabeth* on the West side."

Queen Elizabeth at St. Dunstan-in-the-West

"Then is Staple Inne, also of Chancery, but whereof so named I am ignorant: the same of late is for a great part therof fayre builded, and not a little augmented: And then at the Barre endeth this ward without newgate."

Wednesday, June 23, 1976

Another very warm morning. Bob and I travelled together on the bus to Gray's Inn Road and there we separated, he to the library and I to sketch in the area. My first sketch was Staple Inn, Holborn, the Elizabethan houses of 1586. These houses front on Holborn (the Inn is behind them), and are at Holborn Bars. This is where two Griffins, mounted on stone pedestals, mark the City boundary line. The Inn is one of the Inns of Court dating from the fourteenth century when it was a place for England's wool traders. I tried to sketch the whole picture, houses and Griffins and Holborn. It was complicated and took me until past noon. By this time Holborn was very busy with the lunchtime crowds and I was glad I'd started early.

Staple Inn, Holborn

Monday, April 8, 1974

Today on Fleet Street I found a good art store and bought some colored pencils. English pencils have such lovely subtle colors that suit the London scene better than our bright ones. I wandered around the area searching for a place that I could sketch quickly just to try the pencils. I found it, a charming archway, down a narrow alley near St. Dunstan's Church. Above it was carved a coat of arms and the words "Clifford's Inn." When I got back to the flat Bob told me that Clifford's Inn used to be an Inn of Court. After the Great Fire of 1666, many lawsuits were settled here, lawsuits having to do with claims of property lost in the Fire. All this I just happened to stumble onto in today's wandering!

"Next beyond this church is Cliffords Inne, somtime belonging to *Robert Clifford*, by gift of *Edward* the second. . . . After the death of this *Robert Clifford*, *Isabel* his wife let the same messuage to Students of the law. . . .

This house hath since fallen into the kinges hands, as I haue heard, but returned againe to the *Cliffordes*, and is now letten to the said Studentes for foure pound by the yeare."

Clifford's Inn

170

"Then is the Parish church of Saint Bridges, or Bride, of olde time a small thing, which now remaineth to be the quire, but since encreased with a large bodie and side lles, towards the West, at the charges of *William Venor* Esquire, Warden of the Fleete, about the yeare 1480 all which he caused to be wrought about in the stone in the figure of a vine with Grapes and leaues, &c."

Saturday, October 13, 1984

Walked along Fleet Street this morning and stopped in to one of my favorite churches, St. Bride's. The name comes from St. Bridget, a stone church that was built here in the sixth century and named for the Irish saint. Wren rebuilt this church over the remains of six earlier churches. The bombing of 1940 opened up the way for excavation and discovery of these early remains. Fourteen hundred years of history can be seen in the crypts, it's a dramatic presentation. I was especially interested in the early printing history of St. Bride's. Caxton's apprentice, Wynkyn de Worde, had his printing press alongside this church. He was buried here in 1535 and in his will he left one pound a year for the poor of the parish. For over four hundred years Fleet Street has been home to the press. St. Bride's is their church.

Ten years ago I visited these crypts. Today I was anxious to see them again. I walked along the Roman pavement and I sketched the medieval chapel, the same one I'd done in 1974. I think this drawing is the better one, even though it was very dark and hard to see in there. I was glad to be alone in the chapel. It seemed almost like a prayer, drawing in that ancient place.

Chapel under St. Bride's

172

"These knights Templars tooke their beginning about the yeare 1118 in maner following. Certaine Noble men, horsmen, religiously bent, bound by vow themselues in the handes of the Patriarke of *Ierusalem*, to serue Christ after the manner of Regular Canons in chastitie and obedience, and to renounce their own proper willes for euer.... Their first profession was for safegarde of the Pilgrimes comming to visite the sepulchre, and to keepe the high wayes agaynst the lying in wayte of theeues. . . . Many Noble men in all partes of Christendome became Brethren of this order, and builded for themselues Temples in euerie Citie or great Towne in England, but this at London was their chiefe house."

Thursday, April 4, 1974
The Victoria Embankment is always interesting, fast moving traffic and slow moving pedestrians. The Thames is a working river here. Today it was pale olive green in the noonday sun. Construction cranes were swinging through the sky. Along the riverbank, much activity and noise. On the other side of the road Inner Temple, one of the Inns of Court, looked quiet and serene, green grass bordered by brick buildings and great black trees twisting and curving to the sky. Barristers were strolling two by two along the paths, looking rather grave in their black jackets and striped trousers. Before the Embankment was built these gardens extended to the river. The barristers used to have a private steam packet transport them to the law courts. Now of course, the Law Courts are neighbors.

Inner Temple from the Embankment

"These knights had their head house for England by west Smithfield . . . but they resort all to the said Temple Church, in the round walke whereof (which is the West part without the Quire) there remaineth monuments of Noblemen buried, to the number of 11 eight of them are Images of armed knights, fiue lying crosse legged as men vowed to the holy land, against the infidels . . . the first of the crosse legged was *W. Marshall* the elder Earle of Pembrooke, who dyed 1219 *Wil. Marshall* his sonne Earle of Pembrooke was the second, he died 1231 and *Gilbert Marshall* his brother, Earle of Pembrooke, slayne in a Turnement at Hertford, besides Ware, in the yeare 1241."

Thursday, May 21, 1981

I walked over to Temple Church (my first visit this trip), one of the City's most spectacular churches. I wanted to see if the effigies were the same ones John Stow wrote about, and they were. The Marshall family was still there! I sketched some of the cross-legged knights. These are supposed to be knights who were in the Crusades. This is questionable, but I like to believe it is true. These stone knights were damaged in the Blitz and carefully repaired. Defaced as they are, they still evoke a strange feeling of the strength and power of medieval soldiers, beautiful in their sleep of stone. I stayed on after sketching. Had a delightful chat with a visitor from Suffolk, and then I bought a floor plan of the church and was given a short tour.

Effigies at the Temple Church

Sundial, Inner Temple

Thursday, October 11, 1984

The sun actually shined today! I took a bus down to St. Clement Danes and found the light was wrong for sketching there. Walking to the bus stop I saw Essex Street, named for the Earl of Essex who lived there in banishment. I couldn't resist walking down this street. Essex House used to stand here, originally the town house of the See of Exeter. Somewhere I've read that Nicholas Throckmorton died here, possibly poisoned. Well, it was just an ordinary street today, despite all its ghosts, but it did lead to an entrance to Middle Temple. All was quiet and beautiful in there, lush greens, intriguing walks, and old buildings. I wanted to stop and sketch, but I wanted to explore too. Kept moving farther and farther along until I came to Inner Temple Garden. It was lunchtime, and people were strolling around the lovely green. I ventured in and sat on a bench to do a drawing of a sundial. This was close by a place where red and white roses grow. Padre Thomas once told me that these roses were the symbols of the Yorkists and Lancastrians who fought the Wars of the Roses—the white rose of York, and the red rose of Lancaster. My father came from Lancashire. I wear a little red rose on my charm bracelet.

"These knights . . . granted (for a certayne rent of x pound by the yeare) the said Temple with the appurtenances therevnto adioyning, to the students of the common lawes of England: in whose possesion the same hath euer sithence remained, and is now diuided into two houses of seuerall students, by the name of Innes of Court, to wit, the Inner Temple and the middle Temple, who kept two seuerall halles."

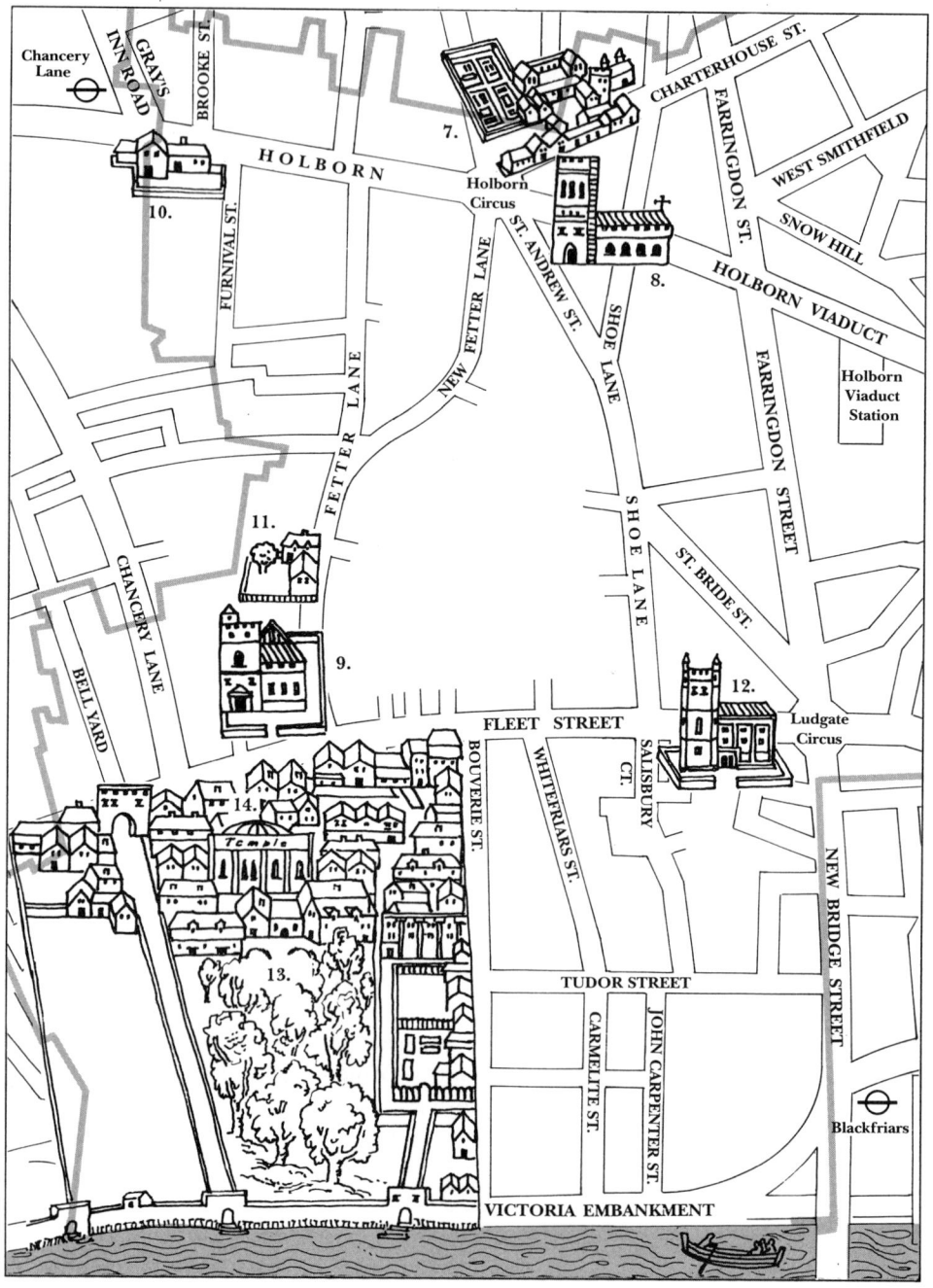

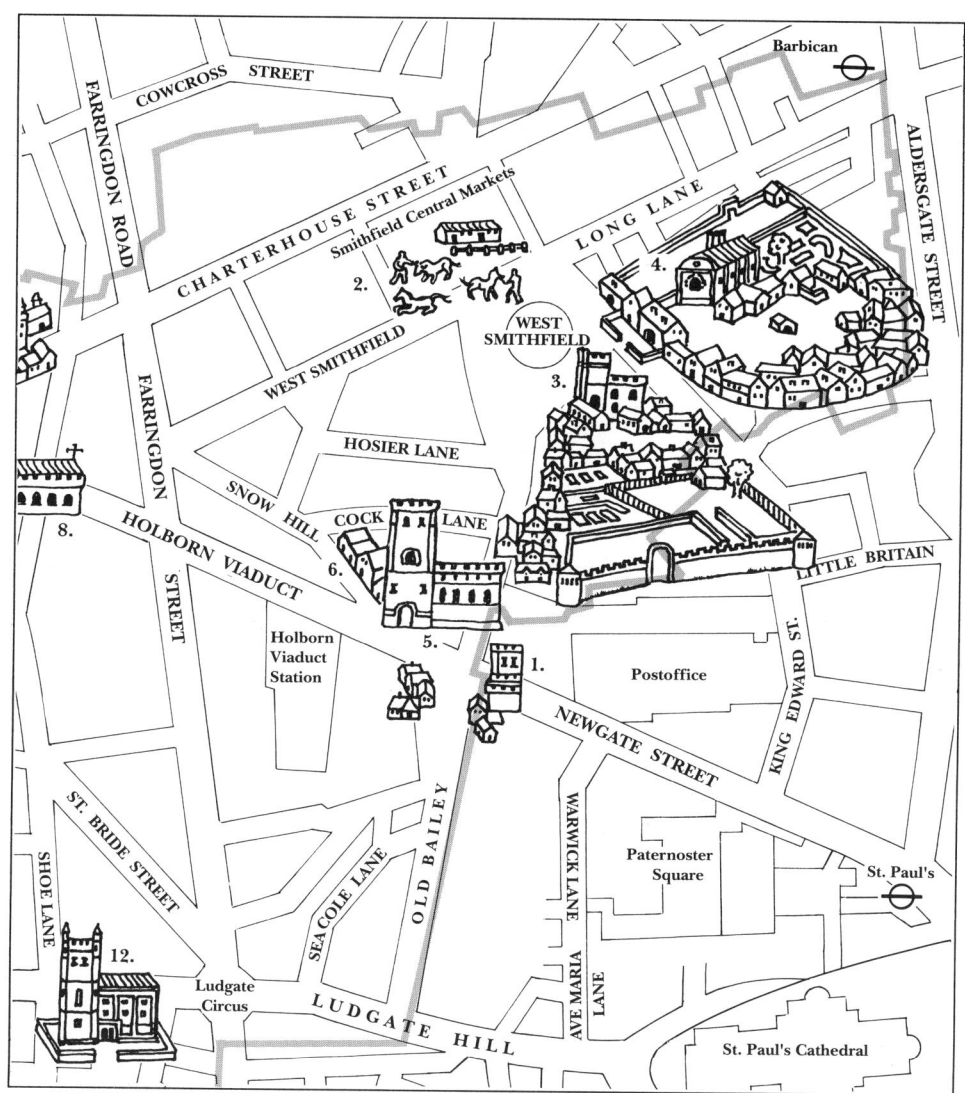

FARINGDON WARDE WITHOUT

1. Newgate, (Old Bailey)
2. Smithfield
3. Church of St. Bartholomew-the-Less
4. Church of St. Bartholomew-the-Great
5. Church of St. Sepulchre-without-Newgate
6. Saracen's Head Inn
7. Church of St. Etheldreda, Ely Place

8. Church of St. Andrew, Holborn
9. Church of St. Dunstan-in-the-West
10. Staple Inn
11. Clifford's Inn
12. St. Bride's Church
13. Inner Temple
14. Temple Church

Note: *The golden boy of Pie Corner is along Cock Lane behind numbers 5 and 6.*
House at Cloth Fair is on Cloth Fair, a street along the north side of St. Bartholomew-the-Great.
Note: *See page ix.*

St. Mary Overie's Dock

26.

"Having treated of Wardes in London, on the North side the Thames (in number 25) I am now to crosse ouer the said Riuer into the Borough of Southwark, which is also a Warde of London, without the walles, on the South side thereof."

Thursday, June 19, 1990

I took the 12:37 train back from York today. That's a very fast train and I got back in time to go over once more to Southwark in the late afternoon. I wanted to sketch the little dock area in back of the Cathedral. This is an amazing area along the Thames. I walked around here in 1974, but the only place I remember from that episode was the little house that Christopher Wren lived in while his Cathedral was being built (and the house is still there). Now, close by Southwark Cathedral, is a small narrow dock with the ship *Kathleen and May* tied up there.

This is St. Mary Overie's Dock, "Overie" meaning "over the water." This dock is sixteenth century, and the sign on the fence said the parishioners of St. Savior's parish were entitled to land goods free of toll.

I spent quite a while sketching the square rigger, ships take so long to do. She is the last British wooden top sail training schooner, built in 1900. I had time to do a quick sketch of another place around the corner from the dock. This was the rose window wall from the banqueting hall of the palace of the Bishop of Winchester. In the fourteenth century this hall was one of the longest great halls in England. It is quite an experience to suddenly come upon this huge stone wall, standing alone and rearing up into the rather grim area of Clink Street.

Clink Street is named for that famous prison dating from 1135 that once stood here. The Clink Museum is on the site of the prison and the palace, and of course I had to go in. It is a scary place with its relics and old prints, but I liked its coat of arms of a sword, keys, and linked hearts representing the palace, the prison and the many brothels of the area.

The next is the Clinke, a Gayle or prison for the trespassers in those parts, Namely in olde time for such as should brabble, frey, or breake the Peace on the saide banke, or in the Brothell houses, they were by the inhabitantes there about apprehended, and committed to this Gayle, where they were straightly imprisoned.

"Next is the Bishoppe of Winchesters house, or lodging when hee commeth to this Cittie: which house was first builded by *William Gifford* Bishoppe of Winchester, about the yeare 1107."

The Rose Window, Bishop of Winchester's Palace

Southwark Cathedral

Monday, October 15, 1984
A misty morning. Took a number 501 bus over to
Southwark Cathedral. A brand new view of the Cathedral
has opened up. The land between the Cathedral and the
Thames is being developed and now there is a fine view
from the Thames side. I sat along Bankside on the stone
steps to paint this beautiful old church. Of course it has

*Wooden bosses
at Southwark Cathedral*

"East from the Bishop of Winchesters house directly ouer against it, standeth a fayre church called saint *Mary* ouer the Rie, or Ouerie, that is ouer the water. This Church or some other in place thereof was of old time long before the conquest an house of sisters founded by a mayden named *Mary,* vnto the which house and sisters she left (as was left to her by her parents) the ouersight and profites of a Crosse ferrie or trauerse ferrie ouer the Thames, there kept before that any bridge was builded. . . .

There be monumentes in this church of . . . *Thomas Cure* Esquier, Sadler to King *Edward* the sixte, Queene *Mary* and Queene *Elizabeth,* deceased the 24 of May, 1588 &c."

been restored many times but much that is ancient is still there. Mist and a damp grayness engulfed the church, the river and me. Cries of sea gulls and faint voices from the excursion boats mixed together with the noise of the bridge traffic and it seemed achingly lovely to me as I worked.

By noontime, however, I was cold and wet. I remembered that when I was here in 1976 one could get a cup of tea in the Cathedral at lunchtime, so I climbed the well worn steps up to the bridge and back down again to the Cathedral yard. There used to be a sun dial in this yard. I'll always remember its inscription, "Time wanes awaye as fflowres decay." It wasn't there today, and no tea either. But I did see the effigy of Thomas Cure Esq. that John Stow mentioned. There he was, a carving of an emaciated figure wrapped in a shroud. He was probably one of the Augustinian canons of the priory of St. Mary Overie, according to the description given, and it said that our ancestors did not shrink to show death as it really was. They were right. I was not quite up to sketching Thomas.

I did something more lively, two of the group of twelve wooden bosses at the back of the church. These came from the roof of the fifteenth century church. John Stow would have seen them as he gazed upward. There were 150 bosses in an oak roof that replaced the earlier thirteenth century stone roof. When these bosses were taken down in 1830, a few of them were saved and they are a fascinating example of the woodcarvers' art.

I ended my visit to Southwark Cathedral with some quiet moments in John Harvard's Chapel, and then walked across the bridge to Fishmongers Hall in time to take their tour. This ended about three o'clock. Coming out of the hall, I had a sudden inspiration to retrace my steps to Southwark and wash in some color on my drawing, though it was still misty and gray.

Tuesday, June 5, 1990

This has been another great day. After breakfast at St. Margaret's Hotel, Mr. and Mrs. Marazzi, the proprietors, urged me to stay around a few minutes because the choir from William and Mary College in Virginia was going to sing a goodby to the hotel. They stayed here during their London visit. The young voices started the day off beautifully. I took the tube to London Bridge and found my way over to Southwark Cathedral through that maze of traffic and construction that seems to be always around this station. I intended to spend a little time renewing my acquaintance with the Cathedral but the sight of some very old arches just inside the entrance was not to be denied. I stopped right there and did a watercolor of this thirteenth century corner of the church John Stow knew as St. Mary Overie.

When I left the Cathedral I still had time to wander around the neighborhood. What surprises there are along the Thames to the northwest! I must get back here soon.

Thirteenth century arches, Southwark Cathedral

Tuesday, June 29, 1976

Bob told me about an old inn called "The George" over in Southwark. He thought I should sketch it because it's one of the last galleried inns left in London. I went over to Southwark today and walked along Borough High Street until I found an "indentation," a most unlikely alley, but it led to this marvelous old inn. It was a little late in the lunch hour. Most of the customers were leaving but there was one young woman who sat alone in the yard drinking beer. Not quite sure how I was going to sketch this inn, I walked the length of the alley-like yard and at the very end was a red leather sofa! I couldn't resist. I did my drawing from there. Lots of cats around, none friendly.

This inn was rebuilt in 1677. Dickens stayed here and Shakespeare may have. I could imagine his players performing in this yard while the audience watched from the galleries above. I left about quarter to four and bussed across the London Bridge to the Bank and on to Selfridge's to get something for supper. Another bus and I was back at the flat in Maida Vale at five forty-five. Bob was waiting and a bit anxious about me, but he liked my drawing.

"From thence towards London bridge on the same side, be many fayre Innes, for receipt of trauellers, by these signes, the Spurre, Christopher, Bull, Queenes head, Tabarde, George, Hart, Kinges Head, &c."

The George in Southwark

St. Thomas's Tower

Friday, August 6, 1976

Not feeling too great this morning, but I did not want to waste any more precious time. I went over to Southwark and along St. Thomas's Street to do the brick tower of St. Thomas's Church. It is a strong, dark tower, a powerful presence on this street. A nineteenth-century operating theatre, the oldest surviving in Britain, is at the top of the tower. The narrow circular staircase was a wicked one, but I made it on the second try, lugging my gear with me. It opened onto a small room where the attendant waited to collect my 25 pence. To allay his suspicions over my large straw bag, I showed him the watercolor I'd just done. He was so pleased he became my personal guide, telling me the history of this surprising place. St. Thomas's Church was the parish church inside the old St. Thomas's hospital. It was rebuilt by Thomas Cartwright, Christopher Wren's master mason, when Wren was a hospital governor. No wonder I was attracted to the tower. He probably had more than a bit of influence on the design of this church.

". . . the hospitall of Saint *Thomas*, first founded by *Richard* Prior of Bermondsey, in the Selerers ground agaynst the wall of the Monasterie in the yeare 1213. . . . In the yeare 1552 the Citizens of London, hauing purchased the voyde suppressed Hospitall of Saint *Thomas* in Southwarke, in the Moneth of Iuly, began the reparations thereof, for poore, impotent, lame, and diseased people."

St. Thomas's herb garret

The operating theatre dates from the early nineteenth century. It is a small round room with four levels for spectators, a tiny operating table, and two chairs. One chair was for the doctor for "low operations," and the other a delicate horsehair seat for important visitors. This operating theatre was for women, and was first used before there were antiseptics or anaesthetics. I wondered how many patients survived their operations.

A much more cheerful place was the herb garret above the church. This is where the medicines were prepared and herbs were dried. Even today it has a delightfully dry, pungent smell, and the intricate beams were a pleasure to sketch.

The church is no longer used. The hospital moved from here in the 1870's and now is located in Lambeth across the river from Westminster. The church buildings are now the Chapter House of Southwark Cathedral. Today was an unexpected treat. A real day of discovery, and to think I almost missed it because the stairs were so steep to climb!

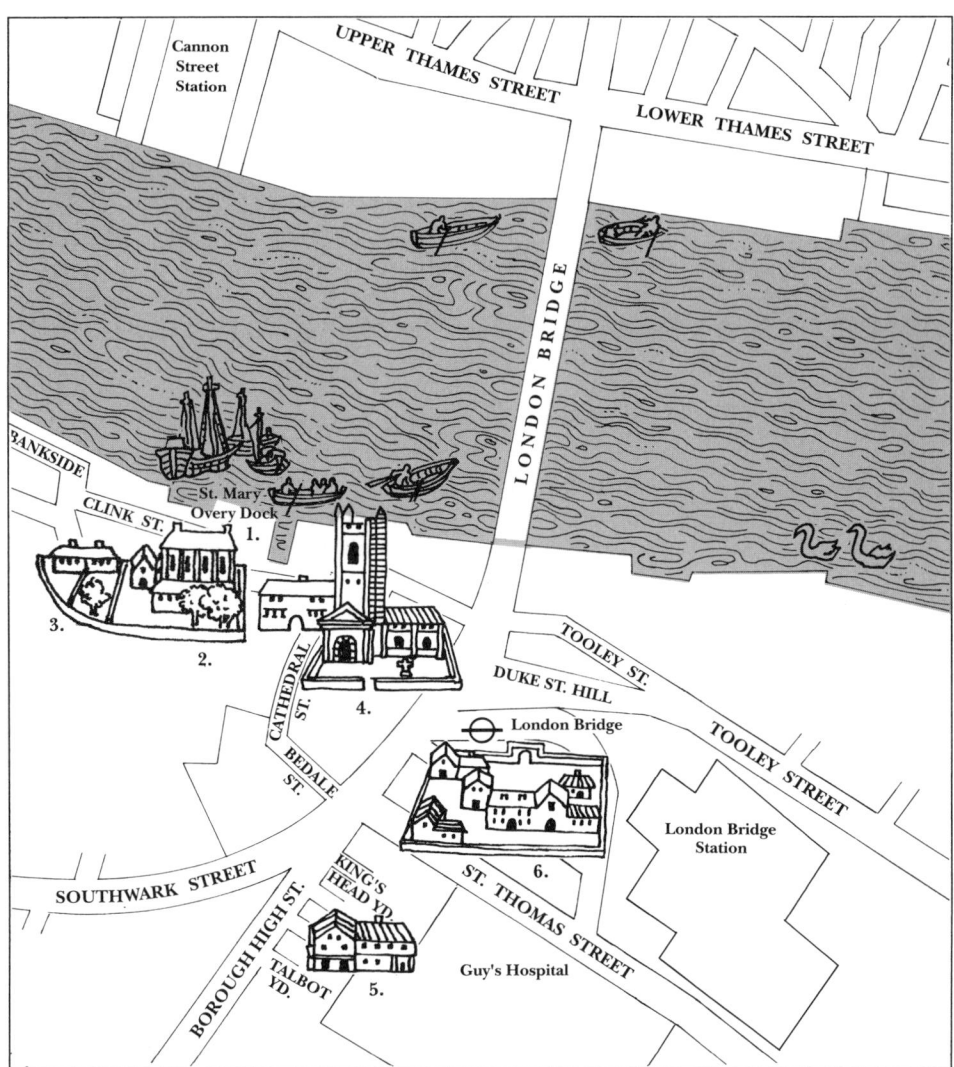

BOROUGH OF SOUTHWARKE AND BRIDGE WARDE WITHOUT

1. St. Mary Overie's Dock
2. Bishop of Winchester's Palace
3. The Clink
4. Southwark Cathedral
5. The George
6. St. Thomas Church and Hospital

27.

"Hauing spoken of this citie, the originall, & increase, by degrees. . . . I am next to speake briefly of the Suburbs, as wel without the gates, & wals, as without the liberties."

"Now for the Parrish of S. Leonards at Soersditch, the Archdeacon of London is alwayes Parson thereof, and the Cure is serued by a Vicar. In this church haue beene diuers honourable persons buried. . . . Notwithstanding that of late one Vicker there, for couetousnes of the brasse which he conuerted into coyned siluer, plucking vp many plates fixed on the graues, & left no memory of such as had beene buried vnder them: A greate iniurie both to the liuing and the dead, forbidden by publike proclamation, in the raigne of our soueraigne Lady Queene *Elizabeth,* but not forborn by many, that eyther of a preposterous zeale, or of a greedy minde spare not to satisfie themselues by so wicked a meanes."

Friday, April 16, 1974

Some sunshine, even though the air stayed cool, sent me to Shoreditch today to do another nursery rhyme church, St. Leonard's. "When I grow rich, say the bells of Shoreditch," and it must mean St. Leonard's Church. Its bells were famous. It's said that Queen Elizabeth loved to hear them ring. Its early parish register records the names of many actors from the two theatres nearby, the "Theatre" and "Curtain" of Shakespeare's time.

St. Leonard's was rebuilt by George Dance the Elder in the 1730's on the site of a twelfth century church. It's big and solid with a very tall steeple topped by a slender spire. I sat on the west side of High Street to do my sketch. Friendly people stopped to look. An old man said "Why don't you wait till it's warmer?" Another man admired my drawing and then asked me where the American Embassy was. As it happened, I did know because Bob and I often go over to Grosvenor Square for an evening walk, and the embassy is very much a part of that square.

After I finished I walked down Bishopsgate and had a sausage on a roll and a cup of tea in a small shop run by a woman and her young daughter. Her grandfather cleared a table for me. They were all friendly. A very nice morning.

St. Leonard's Church in Shoreditch

Finsbury Square, northwest corner

"This fielde of old time was called the More. . . . This Fen or More field stretching from the wall of the City betwixt Bishopsgate and the posterne called Cripples gate to Fensbery . . . continued a wast and vnprofitable ground a long time. . . .In the yeare 1498 all the Gardens which had continued time out of mind, without Moregate, to witte, aboute and beyonde the Lordship of Finsbery, were destroyed. And of them was made a playne field for Archers to shoote in."

Wednesday, April 15, 1981

A busy morning. Bussed over to the National Theatre to get tickets for "A Month in the Country" for Monday night. Back to the Guildhall area to a small tobacconist to get Bob a pipe for Easter. Then I took a bus along Moorgate to Finsbury, a place that John Stow wrote about. I found the huge Finsbury Square divided in two parts. The greens were beautifully kept and surrounded with handsome borders of trees and flower beds and shrubs. One section was for relaxing on the grass, the other was for looking only. I strolled around for a while, walking north up Tabernacle Street thinking about John's windmills and sure enough, I found a pub called "The Windmill Pub." I'll sketch that another day. Today I wanted to just stroll around. Walking back to Finsbury Square, however, I did do a sketch of the northwest corner. It was rather difficult. It should have some color in it to define the green. Since it was getting late, I left, hoping to come back here again.

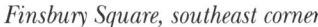

Finsbury Square, southeast corner

The Windmill Pub

Thursday, April 16, 1981

A cool day with sunshine and blue sky. It seemed to be a good day to try (I mean sketch) that pub I saw yesterday. Back to Finsbury again and to Tabernacle Street. This used to be called Windmill Street, and I wondered why they changed the name. I was glad the pub was carrying on the tradition. I sat across the street and worked about three hours and wondered if the patrons knew the history of the windmills the pub was named for. Their drinks might not seem so refreshing! The manager of the pub came over and wanted to buy my drawing, and the man who owned the place came by and asked me if I would sketch other pubs he owned. I took his card and said I'd let him know. I left Tabernacle Street in a good mood.

It was only three o'clock so I went back to the Square to sit in the sun and do a quick sketch of the southeast corner. I was joined by a delightful character who chatted as I worked. He was Irish, Jerry by name, and was "newly from the pubs" (it being after hours). He liked my drawing of the Windmill pub, said he knew it well. I'm sure he did.

"Whereupon in the yeare 1527 sir *Thomas Semor* Mayor caused diuers sluces to be made, to conuey the sayd waters ouer the Towne ditch, into the course of Walbrooke, and so into the Thames: and by these degrees was this Fenne or More at length made main and hard ground . . . also the further groundes beyonde Fensbury Court haue been so ouerheightned with Laystalles of dung, that now three windmilles are thereon set: the ditches be filled vp, and the bridges ouerwhelmed."

Thursday, May 14, 1981

I first found Charterhouse in 1974. It's one of London's charming hidden areas. Today I went there to do a watercolor of the ancient doorway, a doorway that was there when John Stow strolled this area. I sat on the grass just outside the iron fence close by the gate to the park. Some of the gentlemen from Charterhouse passed by quite close to me as they went for their morning walk in the park. I noticed their quick glances and then they politely looked away. Construction workers on their lunch hour were playing soccer nearby and the square

echoed to their shouts. It was pleasant working there and my sketch came out pretty well too.

When I was getting ready to leave I missed my case of pens. The soccer players came by and one of them said, "Is that your wallet, madam?" Sure enough the case lay some distance behind me inside the fence. How it had wandered so far I do not know. I was delighted to find it and thanked him enthusiastically, and was rewarded by a friendly grin. A small thing, but it added to the day's contentment.

"And without the barre of West Smithfield lyeth a large street or way, called of the house of *S. Iohn* there, *S. Iohns* streete, and stretcheth towards Iseldon, on the right hand whereof stoode the late dissolued Monasterie, called the Charterhouse, founded by sir *Walter Manny* knight, a stranger borne, Lord of the towne of Manny in the Dioces of Cambrey, beyond the seas."

Charterhouse gate

Tuesday, October 16, 1984

I have been hunting for Pardon Churchyard by Charterhouse. My research tells me it's no longer there. However, I've studied the maps of the period and it seems to me that it was just north of Charterhouse. This afternoon I walked along Old Street and Clarkenwell Road and found a way into the grounds of the medical college of St. Bartholomew's Hospital, in back of Charterhouse. One of the students told me to see the bursar for permission to sketch there. I found the bursar, who was most cordial. We sat in his office and had a long

chat about the area. He did not agree with me about Pardon Churchyard being here. He suggested I paint the small cells of the monks on the far side of the green. There were too many cars parked alongside to see it clearly, so I sat in the yard and did a view of Charterhouse with the tower. The monk's cells were to the far right. It was a cool misty afternoon and the bare trees and dark colors were exactly right for this aged place. I felt a sadness for those poor people who, so long ago, found their last resting place in a churchyard near here.

"About this in the yeare 1349 the said sir *Walter Manny* in respect of daunger that might befal in this time of so great a plague and infection, purchased thirteene Acres and a rode of ground adioyning to the said *no mans land* . . . and caused it to be consecrated by the said Bishop of London to the vse of burials.

"And the yeare 1371 hee caused there to bee founded an house of Carthusian Monks, . . . he also gaue them the three Acres of land lying without the walles on the North part . . . remained till our time, by the name of Pardon Churchyard, and serued for burying of such as desperately ended their liues, or were executed for Felonies."

Charterhouse from St. Bart's Medical College

Tuesday, April 23, 1974

Still looking for one of the nursery rhyme churches, "Pokers and tongs say the bells of Saint Johns." Today I got as far as St. John's Gate, the marvellous old gateway to the Priory of the Order of St. John. It dates from 1504 and it is a beauty. I sat on my folding stool alongside a shop selling polishers (cloths, chamois, machinery), and started my drawing. Many people stopped to talk to me, including a charming young woman who was the curator of St. John's Museum. She said she would be happy to take me through the church anytime. Three gentlemen also stopped to compliment me on my sketch. They were members of the order, and one was a former Lord Mayor. The shop keeper joined us and there was good natured kidding about his ancestors polishing the armour of the knights. After I finished my drawing I was invited to have a cup of tea with one of the knights. An hour's conversation about politics, education, and the order's work in the health field (they run an ambulance service) sent me home in an euphoric mood.

St. John's Gate

Monday, May 6, 1974

Pamela, the curator of St. John's, took me through the church today. A plain building outside with doors that opened onto a light airy vista. Whitewashed walls and banners in deep reds and golds made vivid slashes of color. Saint John's Church was restored after the Blitz, but the crypt is twelfth century. Absolutely lovely, but too cold to sketch there. Pamela took me into the garden and left me there to do a sketch of the ancient wall of the church. Movement along the top of the cloister wall turned into a shiny black cat who crept along the wall and actually picked his way down the stones and juttings of the church to jump lightly to the grass. Then he saw me, turned, and climbed back the way he had come to vanish over the cloister. I was sorry to see him go. But it was obvious that I had invaded his territory, he'd be back after I left.

"On the left hand also stoode the late dissolued Priorie of saint *Iohn* of Ierusalem in England, founded about the yeare of Christ 1100 by *Iorden Briset* Baron, and *Muriell* his wife, neare vnto Clarkes well besides west Smithfield . . . saint *Iohns* Church . . . was the chiefe seate in England of the religious knights of *S. Iohn* of Ierusalem, whose profession was, besides their dayly seruice of God, to defende Christians agaynst Pagans, and to fight for the Church, vsing for their habite a blacke vpper garment, with a white Crosse on the fore part thereof. . . .

This Priory church and house of saint *Iohn* was preserued from spoyle, or downe pulling so long as king *Henry* the eight raigned, and was imployed as a storehouse for the kings toyles and tents, for hunting, and for the warres, &c."

St. John's Churchyard

Old Hall archway, Lincoln's Inn

In this place . . . *Henry Lacy Earle of Lincolne, Constable of Chester, and Custos of England, builded his Inne, and for the most parte was lodged there: hee deceased in this house in the yeare 1310."*

Friday, February 15, 1974

Waiting for the Public Records Office to open at one o'clock, I strolled along Chancery Lane as far as the Tudor gateway to Lincoln's Inn. This is one of the great Inns of Court (the guide booklet says "an Inn of Court is a non corporate legal society, having the exclusive right of call to the Bar, that is, the conferring of the rank or degree of barrister"). Bob told me that this was one place I must not miss. Going inside, I immediately knew why as I was caught by its enchantment. The lovely courtyards and great trees, the dark red brick of the ancient buildings surrounding the old squares, all very dramatic. I had to stop long enough to do a sketch of the archway between the chapel and Old Hall. Londoners hurried through on their lunch hour errands, and a young bearded man stopped to ask if he might take my picture, "a snap of the drawer" as he put it.

Old Hall, Lincoln's Inn

Saturday, May 18, 1974

A nice warm day. I ate my home-made lunch on the Embankment. Then I walked down Fleet Street to Lincoln's Inn. Did a sketch of one of the Old Buildings, Old Hall, completed in 1493. What a haven this is! Behind locked doors, this being Saturday, existed a solitude of warm sunlight on close-cropped grass, great plane trees casting shadows over old brick and crenelated walls, an occasional visitor with map and camera, and a far-away clicking of a typewriter as some law student worked at a paper. All is serenity and tradition. Law and order should always be as beautiful as this.

"This Lincolnes Inne . . . is now an Inne of Court, retayning the name of Lincolnes Inne as afore, but now lately encreased with fayre buildinges, and replenished with Gentlemen studious in the common lawes."

200

"In the raigne of *H.* the 8 sir *Thomas Louell* was a great builder there, especially he builded the gate house and forefront towards the east."

Friday, June 8, 1976
I spent the morning visiting or looking for art stores. Bought a paint box at Winsor & Newton and looked for an art store on Fleet Street that I'd used in 1974. It was no longer there, having moved to Long Acre. My feet were too tired to hunt for Long Acre, so I went over to Lincoln's Inn Fields to rest a bit. Then I walked through the old gatehouse and strolled around until I came to a choice bit of garden in back of the library. I sketched an interesting diamond patterned brick house there. The garden is open to the public at lunch time, a nice custom for those who do not belong to the Inn.

Garden at Lincoln's Inn

St. Giles-in-the-Fields

Friday, May 22, 1981
On the way home from a long day of sketching I got off the bus at Centrepoint to see if I could get a drawing of St. Giles-in-the-Fields. There have been three churches built on the site of the old hospital that John Stow wrote about. The present St. Giles dates from 1733. St. Giles was the patron saint of cripples and poor people.

The churchyard yielded no good views and there were no easy places to work from. I was desperate to do it; however, because of John Stow's story of the last bowl of ale for the unfortunate people who stopped there on their way to the gallows at Tyburn. I finally sat along St. Giles Street and sketched the church spire and trees and street corner.

". . . S. Giles in the field, which was an Hospitall founded by *Maltilda* the Queene, wife to *Henry* the first, about the yeare 1117."

"At this Hospitall, the prisoners conuayed from the City of London towardes Teyborne, there to be executed for treasons, fellonies, or other trespasses, were presented with a great Bowle of Ale, thereof to drinke at theyr pleasure, as to be theyr last refreshing in this life."

"Alice La. Hungerford, hanged
at Tiborne for murdering her
husband, 1523."

Thursday, June 18, 1981

I had one more sketch to do before we went home, one
that would complete the story about the prisoners who
journeyed to that dreadful place, the Tyburn Gallows, via
St. Giles-in-the-Fields.

Tyburn was a place of execution for many centuries
until the last gallows hanging there in 1783. The road to
Tyburn was along what is now Oxford Street, today one
of London's largest shopping areas. And Hyde Park
corner, close by the site of Tyburn, is now the place, on
Sunday mornings, of soap box orators and hecklers,
Londoners expressing their opinions. I wonder how
many of them know what once went on there.

It was not far from our flat in Seymour Street, so I
walked over to Hyde Park with my watercolor block. The
gallows used to be near Marble Arch where Edgware
Road meets Bayswater and Oxford Street. I sat on the
grass in Hyde Park facing that area to do a watercolor.
The day was overcast and I felt melancholy as I thought
of days long past when people came here to watch the
hangings. Today was quiet and serene. A sweet damp
smell of new mown grass, faint bird calls, laughter, and
children's voices mingled with the sound of nearby
traffic. All of this made it hard to believe the history of
Tyburn.

Site of the Tyburn Gallows at Marble Arch

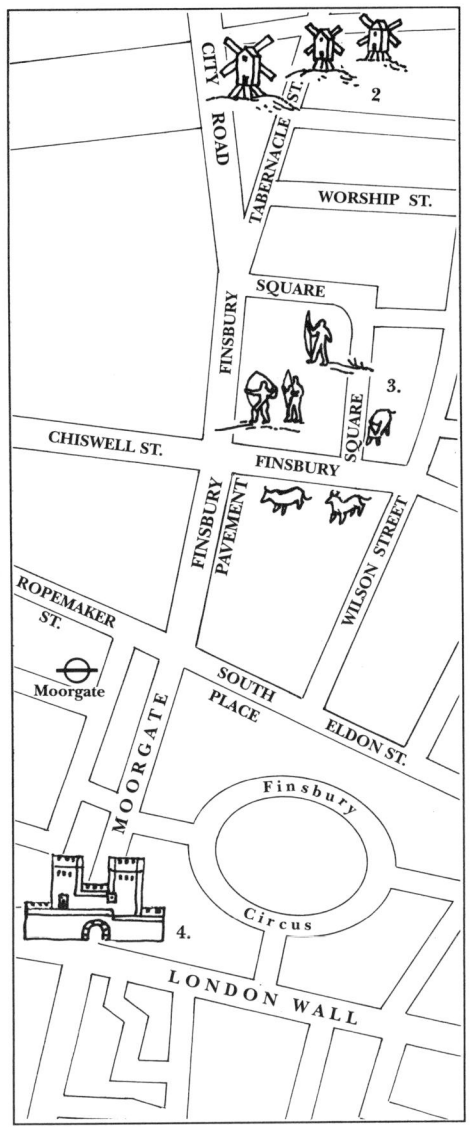

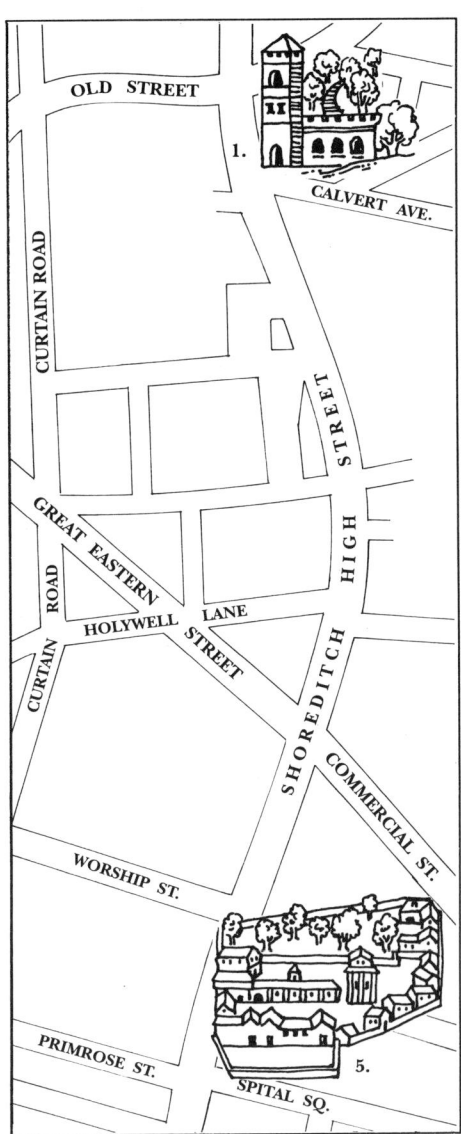

THE SUBURBES WITHOUT THE WALLES

1. Church of St. Leonard, Shoreditch
2. The Windmills at Finsbury
3. Finsbury Fields
4. Moorgate
5 St. Mary Spital Hospital and Priory
   Note: *See page xi and page 129.*

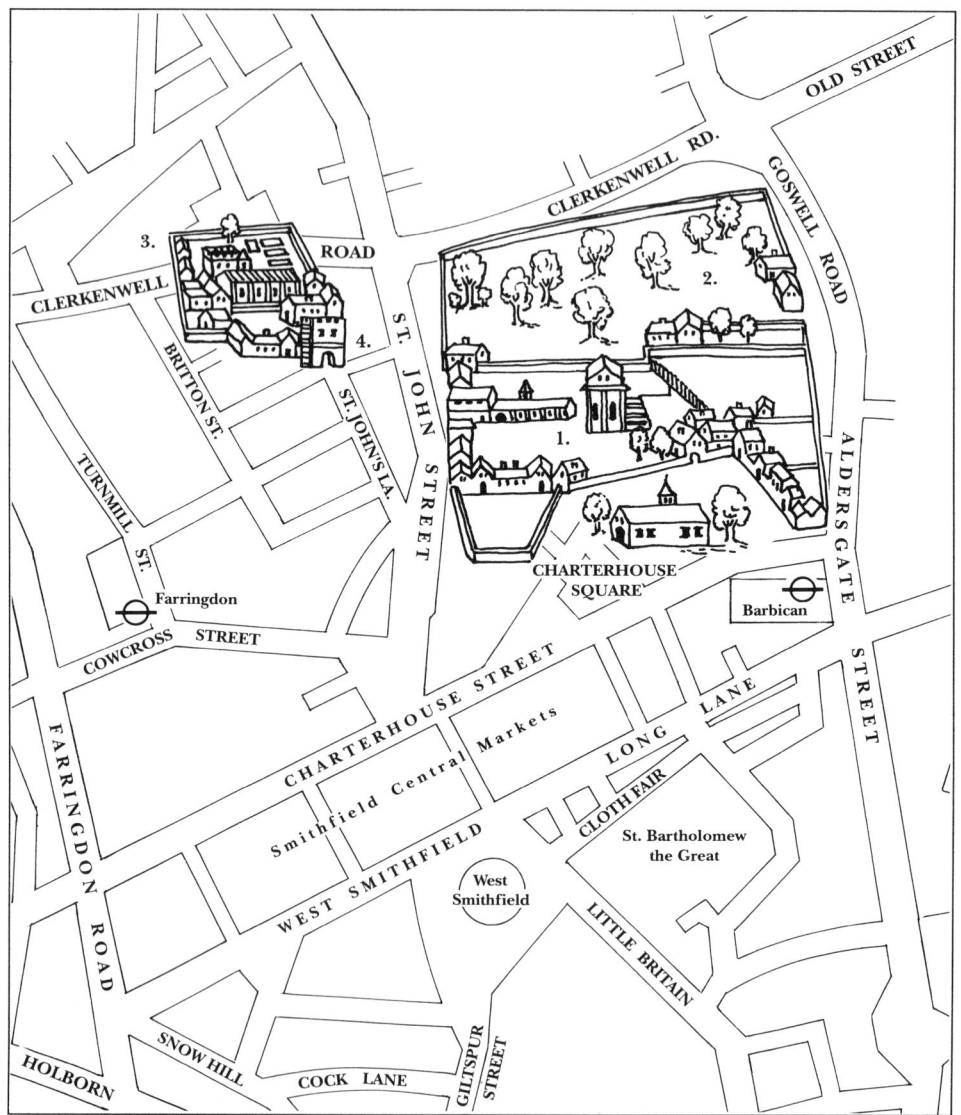

THE SUBURBES continued

1. Charterhouse
2. Pardon Churchyard
3. St. John's Priory and Church
4. Gatehouse of the Order of St. John

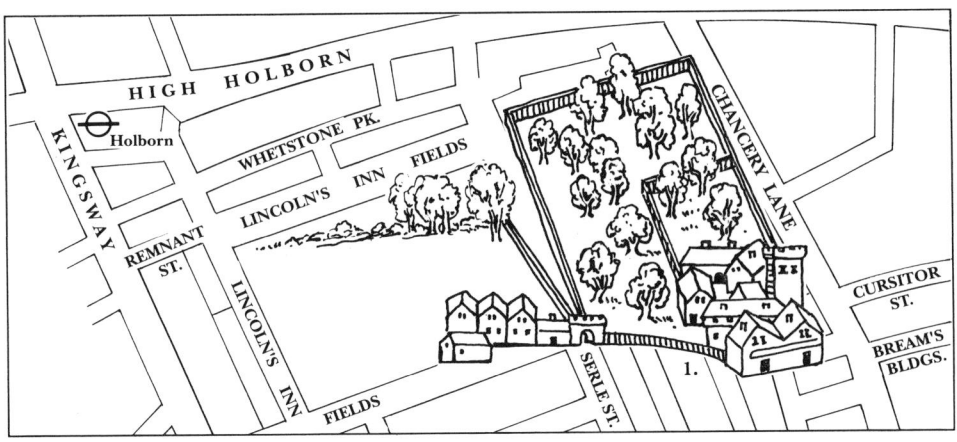

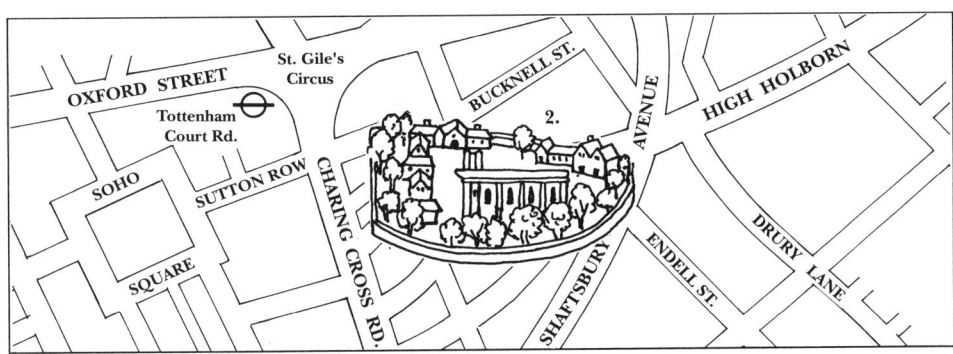

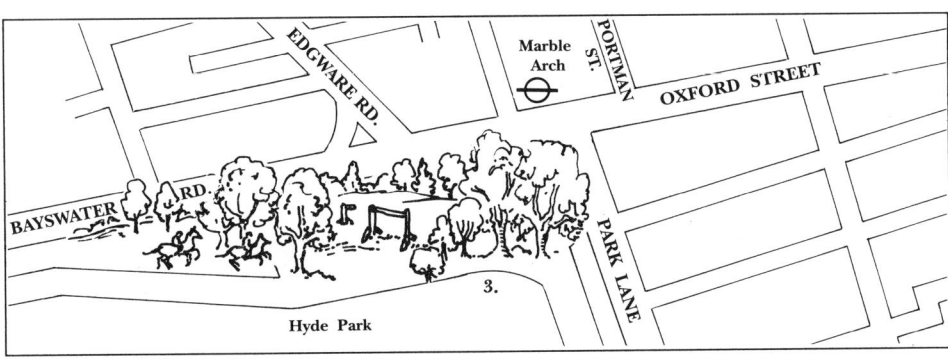

THE SUBURBES continued

1. Lincoln's Inn
2. Church of St. Giles-in-the-Fields
3. Tyburn

28.

"Next without the Barre, the new temple, and Liberties of the Citty of London, in the Suburbes, is a libertie pertayning to the Dutchie of Lancaster."

Monday, October 7, 1991

"This Inne of Chancerie with other houses neare adioyning, were pulled downe in the raigne of *Edward* the 6 by *Edward* Duke of Sommerset, who in place thereof raised that large and beautifull house, but yet vnfinished, called Sommerset House."

This morning I changed some dollars into pounds (a grim procedure), bought a water color pad, and walked over to Somerset House to finish a watercolor I'd started last week. It was one of the old watergates along the Thames. In spite of the heavy traffic along Victoria Embankment, and with lots of patience waiting for clear views, it came out pretty well. Somerset House from the Embankment, and especially from Waterloo Bridge, is one of London's most impressive views. It is an

Somerset House

St. Mary-le-Strand

eighteenth century building designed by Sir William Chambers and later enlarged. The original Somerset House on this site was begun in 1547 for the Duke of Somerset who demolished some fine houses along the Strand and also the little church of St. Mary le Strand in order to build his palace. He died before it was completed. Amen.

I finished the sketch and walked back to St. Mary-le-Strand not far away. This church, on the site of the earlier one, was built by James Gibbs as the first of the fifty new churches to be built under an act of Parliament in 1711 and financed by a coal tax. St. Mary-le-Strand completely captivates me. Sitting in the middle of the street, it seems to preside over the neighborhood. A couple of women, former WRENS, were working in the church and garden. They were a delight to talk with. Old carvings from an earlier church lined the garden pathway, and I chose to draw one little angel who seemed to cry a lament from long ago.

"Next . . . on the street side was sometime a faire cemitorie or churchyeard, and in the same a parish Church called of the Natiuity of our Lady and the Innocents of the Strand, & of some by meane of a Brotherhood kept there, called of S. *Vrsula* at the Strand."

"Then next is the Sauoy, so called of *Peter* Earle of Sauoy and Richmond. . . . He first builded this house in the yeare 1245. . . . This house . . . of latter time came to the kings hands, and was again **rays**ed and beautifully build-**ed**, for an Hospitall of *S. Iohn Baptist,* by king *Henry* the seuenth, about the yeare 1509. . . . The Chappell of this Hospitall serueth now as a Parish church to the Tene-ments thereof neare ad-ioyning and others."

Friday, October 19, 1984

After many attempts I finally got in to the Savoy Chapel today and managed to get a sketch of this famous place. Sitting in the churchyard I did a drawing of the Queen's Chapel of the Savoy, "the chapel of the Sovereign in right of the Duchy of Lancaster." It is all that remains of the chapel founded by Henry VII, which first served as a hospital and almshouse. Only the north walls and side are original. When I finished, the verger took me into the Chapel and turned on the lights. The unique charm of this small chapel glowed in the soft light. It has a pearwood ceiling, reconstructed after the Blitz. There are sixteen royal stalls, the two in the center for the Sovereign and the Grand Master of the Royal Victorian Order. The verger and I were delighted to find we both came from Lancashire, my route being a little more round about than his. It turned out to be a most pleasant day.

Savoy Chapel

St. Clement Danes

Monday, June 3, 1974
Household chores most of the day. The laundromat, packing books to send home, and marketing. John and Enid Thomas, the chaplain of St. Clement Danes and his wife, are coming to dinner tomorrow. They had mentioned that they would like a sketch of the church, so after an early supper I went down to do some drawings of this beautiful RAF church.

Like many famous places, St. Clement Danes has its share of legend and history. When Alfred the Great drove the Danes from London, he allowed those who had taken

"Now to beginne againe at Temple Barre ouer against it. In the high streete as is afore shewed, is one large Middle Rowe of houses and small Tenementes builded, partly opening to the South, partlie towardes the north. Amongst the which standeth the parrish Church of saint *Clement Danes,* so called because *Harolde* a Danish king and other Danes were buried there."

English wives to remain and live just outside the City on the way to Westminster. There they built a church and named it for St. Clement, who was the patron saint of mariners. Around 1022 a stone church replaced the old wooden one, and the church booklet says its remains are in the present tower. This church was built at the very center of London's history, on the road from the City to Westminster, so it couldn't fail to be enveloped in the dramatic and sometimes bloody action that went on for many centuries. It escaped the Great Fire, but those times were not kind to the church. The Fire and the Plague wiped out much of the population, and St. Clement Danes fell into ruin. Christopher Wren to the rescue! He rebuilt the church, all except the steeple, which was added a little later by James Gibbs. This steeple and the walls were the only parts left after fire bombs destroyed St. Clement Danes one May night in 1941. The church was restored and reconsecrated in 1958, having been returned to its former splendor by the RAF, allied airforces, and friends. It is now the RAF church.

It was very pleasant there this early evening, sitting alongside Australia House with a good view of St. Clements at the end of the Strand. The clear, sharp outlines in the still air, the quiet, almost empty street with just a few theatre-goers hurrying to a seven-thirty curtain, the long shadow of someone stopping behind me to look over my shoulder, all gave the evening a special ambience.

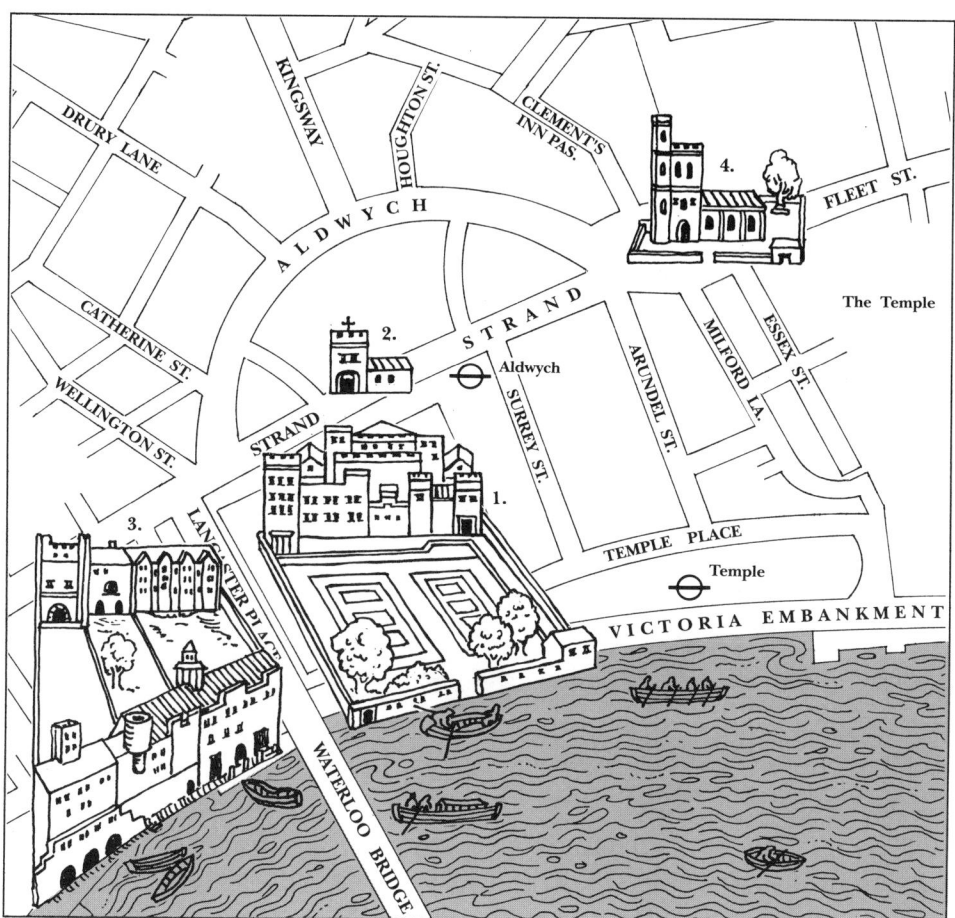

LIBERTIES OF THE DUTCHIE OF LANCASTER

1. Somerset House
2. Church of St. Mary-le-Strand
3. Savoy Palace and Chapel
4. St. Clement Danes Church

St. Martin-in-the-Fields

29.

"Now touching the City of Westminster, I wil beginne at Temple Barre, on the right hand or North side, and so passe vppe West."

Wednesday, May 1, 1974

Bob left for Birmingham this morning. Always that lonesome feeling when he leaves, but it doesn't last very long in London. So much to do and see! Trafalgar Square with rain clouds and rain drops, city workers eating their lunch around the lions and Lord Nelson. The man who stopped to watch me sketching St. Martin-in-the-Fields, saying, "You are a professional, aren't you?" When I nodded he said, "So am I. I am an actor." and strode away before I had a chance to ask him where he might be playing. St. Martin-in-the-Fields was built by James Gibbs, a pupil of Wren's. It is on the site of the early church. Today it is hard to imagine that there were once open fields here!

"From thence is now a continuall new building of diuers fayre houses, euen vp to the Earle of Bedfords house lately builded nigh to Iuy Bridge, and so on the north side to a lane that turneth to the parish Church of S. *Martins* in the field, in the liberty of Westminster."

Sunday, November 3, 1991

From my very first bus ride through this area I'd wondered at the intricate sculpture of the monument standing in front of Charing Cross station. Then later, when I read John Stow, I realized that this was one of the crosses that Edward I erected to mark the place where his beloved queen's funeral cortege had stopped to rest on its journey to Westminster. Of course this cross is a Victorian replica of the original which was destroyed in 1647. The actual site of Eleanor's cross is where the bronze statue of Charles I now stands in Trafalgar Square.

I managed to find a space for myself in the station courtyard, a bit away from the streams of people crossing in front of me. Even so I had a few people stop to watch me sketch. I had good luck with the drawing and finished in plenty of time to walk down to St. Clement Danes for the morning service. Along the Strand I passed many people sleeping in doorways, wrapped in sleeping bags and blankets. Modern London suddenly came alive and took away the euphoria of the past hour.

Tuesday, September 19, 1992

I wanted to sketch the place where Eleanor's Cross originally stood. So, off to Trafalgar Square to do a quick drawing of Charles I astride his horse at the top of Whitehall. I almost caused a traffic jam trying to get over to the small island where Charles and his horse have marked the place since 1675. Surely this must be one of London's earliest statues.

"Neare vnto this Hospitall was an Hermitage, with a chappell of S. *Katherine*, ouer against Charing crosse, which crosse, builded of stone, was of old time a fayre peece of worke there made by commandement of *Edward* the first, in the 21 yeare of his raigne, in memorie of *Helianor* his deceased Queene, as is before declared."

Charles I at Trafalgar Square

Charing Cross on a Sunday morning

St. Jame's Palace

Wednesday, March 6, 1974

Last Sunday's walk with Bob through St. James's Palace was so wonderful that I went back there today to do a sketch. The Gurkhas were still on guard. I think they are terrific. Bob says they are noted for their competence, pride and toughness. I was lucky enough to see the changing of the guard. Very impressive, the stamp of marching feet, the hoarse commands of the officer ringing out in the quiet courtyard, the tense long wait between commands, then the small group marching away, the sound of their boots on the cobblestones growing fainter and fainter.

A shiny black carriage drawn by a beautiful white horse came past me. I could see the coachman, young and erect in a fawn colored Edwardian greatcoat. The passenger, on the other hand, was disappointingly ordinary looking as he ran back and forth from the coach to the various offices. Then they drove out, clappety-clap, to Green Park. All this happened while I was sketching Ambassador's Court. It is a medley of Tudor brick walls and cobblestones. The old chapel, part of Henry VIII's palace, is here but was not open to visitors.

". . . an Hospitall of saint *Iames* . . . founded by the Citizens of London, before the time of any mans memory, for 14 sisters maidens that were leprouse, liuing chastly and honestly in diuine seruice. . . .

This Hospitall was surrendred to *Henry* the eight, the three and twentieth of his raigne, the sisters being compounded with were allowed Pensions for tearme of their liues, and the king builded there a goodly Mannor, annexing thereunto a Parke . . . now called saint *Iames* Parke."

King Sebert's tomb

"And now to passe to the famous Monastery of Westminster: . . . This Monastery was founded and builded by *Sebert* king of the East Saxons, vpon the perswasion of *Ethelbert* king of Kent, who hauing embraced christianity, and being baptized by *Melitus* Bishop of London: immediately (to shew himselfe a christian indeed) built a church to the honour of God and *S. Peter,* on the west side of the city of London. . . . *Edgar* king of the west Saxons repayred this Monastery about the yeare of Christ, 958 E. the Confessor builded it of new. . . . buried in this Church are . . . *Frauncis Sidney* Countesse of Sussex."

Tuesday, September 29, 1992

I can't count the times I've visited Westminster Abbey, but I never feel adequate to the task of sketching there. Today I hoped to find some inspiration, and I did, in the memorials to two of the people John Stow mentions. One was King Sebert, the legendary founder of Westminster Abbey. He died in AD 616 and was buried in his own Abbey church. His tomb is at the entrance to the South Ambulatory. I stood a little ways from the ancient stone and tried to get a quick drawing as a steady flow of visitors filed by. They seemed unimpressed with this simple tomb, after all the brilliance and splendor of the chapels. For me, its simplicity was haunting. The other tomb was one I'd seen before, and it always made me smile. Frances, Countess of Sussex, is in the chapel of Our Lady of the Pew (near the chapel of St. John the Baptist). Graceful and prayerful, she lies with her hands clasped, and at her feet rests a porcupine. Was he a pet? Or part of her coat of arms? Or did he indicate her character? Here too I could only manage a quick sketch in the midst of visitors crowded into this small chapel.

Frances, Countess of Sussex

The Jewel Tower

Just south of the Abbey is the Jewel Tower. A romantic name for one of the last remains of the old Palace of Westminster. It has a little moat around it, and a pretty garden on one side. It is thought to have been built by Henry Yevele, and was the place where Edward III kept his jewels and wardrobe. It has had various uses through the years and is open to the public as a museum. I sketched it one day in 1984 when there were many more visitors around than today. I didn't do it justice. Today was better as I sat on a low retaining wall and did a sepia watercolor. With few people around it was much easier to get closer to the atmosphere of this ancient palace.

"Next to this famous Monastery, is the kings principall Pallace, of what antiquity it is vncertain: but *Edward* the *Confessor* held his court there. . . . The said king had his pallace, and for the most remayned there: where hee also ended his life, and was buried in the Monastery which hee had builded."

St. Margaret's Church, Westminster

Tuesday, September 25, 1984

"He also caused the parish church of *S. Margaret* to be newly builded without the Abbey church of Westminster, for the ease and commodity of the Monks, because before that time the parrish Church stood within the old Abbey church in the south Isle, somewhat to their annoyance."

Spent most of the day around Westminster. In the afternoon I sketched St. Margaret's Church, the parish church of the House of Commons. It sits comfortably alongside the Abbey, sort of protected and yet sturdily independent. William Caxton, printer, and Walter Raleigh, adventurer and friend to Elizabeth I, are buried in this church. That makes St. Margaret's a special place for me.

Tuesday, October 9, 1984

A rainy morning. A good time to start shopping for gifts to take home. Of course shopping took longer than the morning. It was about four-thirty before I got to Parliament Square to do a sketch of Westminster Hall. It was a perfect time to do it. No large crowds in the late afternoon. I was able to relax after a tiring day and sketch without being hurried. This is the Great Hall of the kings of England. Absolutely magnificent. I did it broadside to show the length of the hall and its buttresses. The roof is ninety feet high, a double hammerbeam roof of oak, designed by Henry Yevele, architect to Richard II. Yevele left many masterpieces. This is one of his greatest.

I finished about quarter to six and then strolled around the Dean's yard. So lovely there in the early evening. Got back to St. Margaret's hotel nicely rested and refreshed.

"And it is manifest by the testimonie of many authors, that *W. Rufus* builded the great Hall there, about the year of Christ 1097. . . . A great part of this Palace at Westminster was once againe burnt in the yeare 1512 the 4 of *Henry* the eight, since which time, it hath not beene reedified: only the great Hall, with the offices neare adioyning, are kept in good reparations, and serueth as afore, for feastes at Coronations, Arraignments of great persons charged with treasons, keeping of thc Courts of iustice, &c."

Westminster Hall

"Moreouer in the yeare 1242, the Thames ouerflowing the bankes about Lambhithe, drowned houses and fieldes, by the space of six miles, so that in the great hall at Westminster, men tooke their horses, because the water ran ouer all."

Friday, November 9, 1984

A warmish day with mist and low lying clouds. This might be one of my final days of sketching and I want to do Lambeth Palace. John Stow did not describe Lambeth, but he mentioned it several times. Lambeth Palace is the residence of the archbishops of Canterbury, one of the last remaining medieval bishops' houses in London. My favorite view is from across the Thames, in the Victoria Tower Gardens. In early days most ways to Lambeth were by boat along the river. I could easily imagine the palace I was sketching was the same one John Stow saw when he walked along the river's bank. Thames traffic moved

slowly by and boats were tied up at the jetty in front of Lambeth Palace.

I felt as though I were saying farewell to London this morning. The mist and distance involved made it a simple sketch. It didn't take long to do, but time enough to feel the dampness on my hair. It reminded me of sketching along the Maine coast on a foggy day. There were some gulls perched on the railing in front of me. Of course they were hoping I had my lunch with me. Alas, all I could offer them were greetings from the seagulls back home in Maine.

"*Edmond Boner* Doctor of the ciuill law, Archdeacon of Leycester, then Bishop of Hereford, was elected to London in the yeare 1539. . . . On the first of September 1549 he preached at *Paules* Crosse, for the which sermon he was charged before the counsell of king *Edward* the 6 . . . and being conuented before certain Commissioners at Lambith, was for his disobedience to the kings order, on the 20 day of the same month sent to the Marshalsey and depriued from his bishopricke."

Lambeth Palace from Victoria Gardens

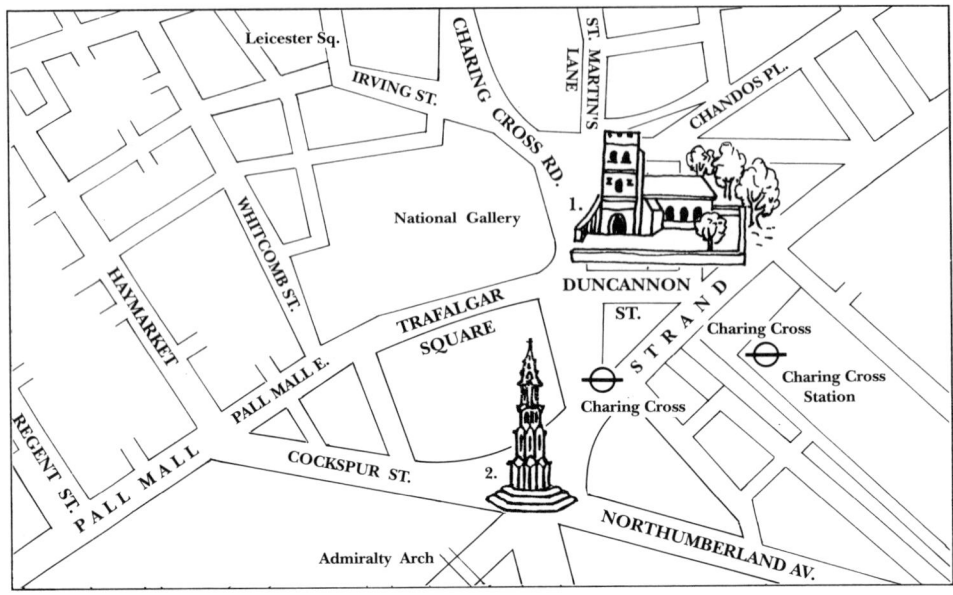

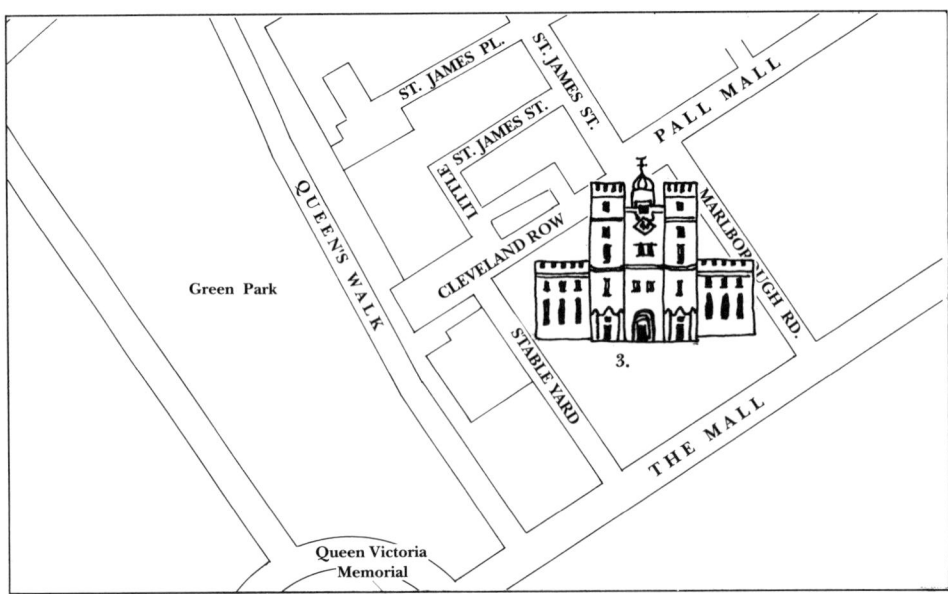

THE CITIE OF WESTMINSTER

1. St. Martin-in-the-Fields Church
2. Charing Cross (original site)
3. St. Jame's Palace

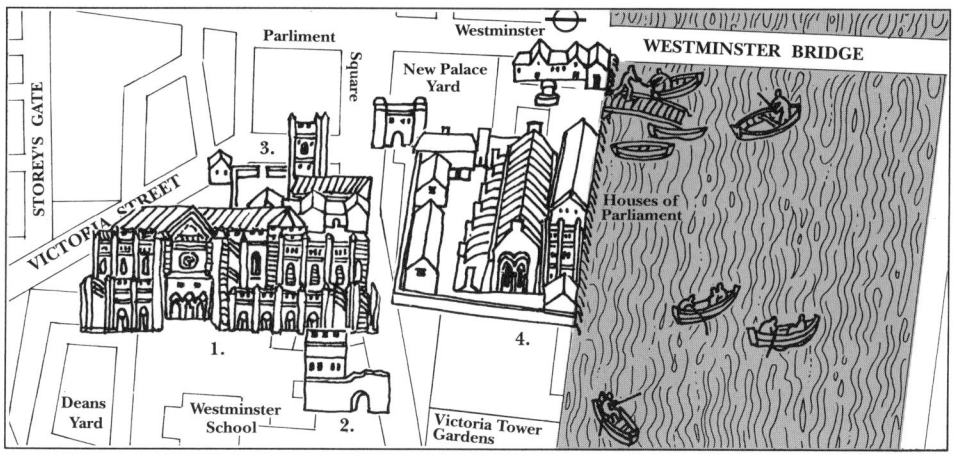

WESTMINSTER continued

1. Monastery of Westminster
2. Jewel Tower, Westminster Palace
3. St. Margaret's Church
4. Great Hall of Westminster
5. Lambeth Palace

Postscript

When my husband and I first arrived in London in 1974, we heard the words, "Hitler's War," in many conversations. Signs of the Blitz were still visible, gaping holes in the ground and buildings sliced open, with rooms and even wallpaper still showing in many places. The huge area north of St. Paul's, the Barbican, was just now in the early stages of reconstruction.

I remember walking around that place and twice getting lost. That year England was plagued with strikes and London was struggling with its brownout. Half the city's lights were dimmed on a limited lighting arrangement to save electricity. Bob was unhappy that I could not see London's lights at night, but the brownout brought its own memorable moments. In our search for an apartment, or 'flat' as I learned to say, we visited an estate agent on Seymour Street. It was a small dark office lit by candlelight, and I remember catching a glimpse of one of the secretaries peering into a telephone directory with a candle dripping wax onto the pages. They were good agents, they found us a delightful flat with a housekeeper who had wonderful stories to tell about the war, and a landlord who became a good friend. Many memories of the brownout remain with me. Buying colored pencils at an art store where I had to carry them to the front window to see the colors, and the dramatic scene in the oriental carpet department of Liberty's where a charmingly costumed Indian woman was weaving a carpet by candlelight. Soft colors and so much atmosphere! Streets were dark at night, but we could go about with no problem so long as we carried a flashlight to read the signs at bus stops. The brownout was lifted in March in time for me to see London's lights before going home.

While I've been sketching the city these past years I've often had construction workers above my head, sometimes calling down compliments or shouting for me to get out of their way. At first, London was repairing and restoring itself after the war. Now however, London, and especially the City, is filling all the spaces and soaring into the skies with exciting architecture. The Barbican and South Bank, East London and the Docks area are places I love to visit, and each time I go there I find more to intrigue me. I could wish for more space for the old churches, such as St. Magnus the Martyr, but then there is St. Giles in its perfect setting in the Barbican. John

Stow lamented about encroachments and crowded conditions in his city, just as we do now. But I think, if he were here today, he'd be pleased to stroll along the Thames embankments, walk through the great parks, and stop to sit and rest in the green squares that seem to be around every other corner in London. These squares are breathing spaces filled with lawns and flower beds, shrubbery and trees, and birds and black iron fences and old statues and benches, where for years Londoners have sat and admired their city.

They have much to admire. Their ancient places are carefully preserved, and their history comes alive everywhere and especially at the very modern Museum of London in the Barbican. It's a pleasure to go through this museum and see the crowds of people with lots of children enjoying their history. I find treasures every time I go there. Only recently I found the handsome oak door from St. Ethelburga's church in the medieval gallery. I can't imagine how I had missed it before. But something was missing, Synagogue had vanished from her glass case in that gallery. I made a nuisance of myself until I was able to speak with someone in the curator's office who assured me that she would soon be back. The statue had been deteriorating and was out for repairs. However, she was still absent when I returned in 1993.

After a long afternoon at the museum, weariness overtook me as I climbed down the stairs to the ground level. There I caught a glimpse of something familiar, a place I'd sketched in 1981. The tiny churchyard of St. Olave, Silver Street was at the foot of the stairs. It gleamed like a jewel that afternoon, with its lush green carpet of newly mowed grass and shiny dark leaved shrubbery. The brick graves and old stone steps had been carefully tended, although the ancient inscriptions were almost worn away. My tiredness vanished, the sight of that old churchyard was as good as a cup of tea.

Another day I walked down Leadenhall to find St. Andrew's Undershaft closed up tight, reminding me of one of my first visits. No signs this time to explain why. I was depressed, but then I came to the Aldgate Pump. A City worker was vigorously polishing the brass rosette and splendid lion's head that adorned the west side of the pump. He said he did this every day except weekends. Seemed as though he liked the pump as much as I did.

The British are well acquainted with their past and fit it easily into the contemporary scene.

I've been fortunate to find family and friends in England, and they have shown me so much more than I could ever find by myself. In Lancashire my father's people opened their hearts to me and made me feel as though I'd always been part of the family. When they showed me the house where he had lived, I was sure I'd seen it before. Of course I had, through the stories he told of his boyhood. In London from Chelsea to East London, in York and Wales, in Oxford and the Cotswolds, in Surrey, Kent and Devon, I found friends who delighted in sharing their lives and showing me their favorite places, and helping me with my research for this book.

In London the first warm welcome by the chaplain of St. Clement Danes and his wife, in 1974, started a long chain of friendship that continues through the years and is renewed each time I return. And, a chance meeting in 1974 with an architect at St. Paul's Cathedral, has led to many exciting excursions into British history. I'm grateful to all of them for enriching my life and my understanding of England and its vibrant past. And now, three cheers for John Stow who started this pleasant and endearing affair.

Acknowledgments

In writing this book, I have often thought of a chance encounter I had in London with Marisa Wright in 1981, when she said, "Don't be discouraged, it will take a few years." How did she know? It has taken more than a few years, and now thanks are due to all my friends and acquaintances for their continued interest and encouragement.

In London, special thanks go to Leo Cooper whose enthusiasm and help have been constant from the very beginning; to Bob Crayford for his lively discussions of architectural history; to everyone at St. Clement Danes, especially Kate Clark and Ethel Cox, two Londoners who know more about the city than most guides, and Pam Baker and Myra Mackay, hospitable friends who enrich my visits each time I come to London. The Museum of London and the Guildhall Library have been invaluable. I am also grateful to the Marazzi family and the staff at St. Margaret's Hotel who have provided me with a "home away from home" whenever I am in London.

In Oxford at Christ Church Library, I found friendly assistance and interest from John Mason, former librarian, and staff members Jennie Bradshaw and John Wing. Jennie has never faltered in her optimism for this work. In York, my friend Freda Alton has shown me many delightful places in England's history. I thank them all.

At home, the University of Maine has sustained me with its appreciation and affection. The exhibitions of my sketches of London, organized by Vincent Hartgen, Huddilston Professor Emeritus of Art, were a starting point of interest for my book.

I am grateful to the friends and neighbors who have supported me all this time, along with those at the university, especially my editor, Matthew Hatvany, and graphic designer colleagues, Michael Mardosa, Carol Nichols, and Valerie Williams whose patience and aid in my computer adventures will always be fondly remembered. For many years I have enjoyed a fine rapport with the University Printing Services and I thank all of them for their interest and fine efforts to satisfy my never ending concerns for the appearance of this book.

I am grateful to Elaine Albright, Dean of Cultural Affairs and Libraries, who has always believed in this diary, and to Fred Hutchinson, President of the University of Maine, and Charles Tarr, Dean of the Graduate School, who caused it to be published.

Appendix

John Stow wrote about William Elderton, an attorney in the sheriff's office, who penned some strangely prophetic verses about the "images of stone" that adorned the porch of the Guildhall. They were removed in 1788, the whereabouts unknown until 1972 when they were found in a garden in North Wales. The statues of the four virtues are now in the Museum of London.

> *Though most the images be pulled down,*
> *And none be thought remayne in Towne,*
> *I am sure there be in London yet,*
> *Seuen images such, and in such a place,*
> *As few or none I thinke will hit:*
> *Yet euery day they shew their face,*
> *And thousands see them euery yeare,*
> *But few I thinke can tell me where,*
> *where Iesus Christ aloft doth stand,*
> *Law and learning on eyther hand,*
> *Disclipline in the Deuils necke,*
> *And hard by her are three direct,*
> *There iustice, Fortitude and Temperance stand,*
> *where find ye the like in all this land?*

Index of Places and Directions for the Nearest Underground Station

(Aldwych Station, open peak hours only, excluded)

Aldersgate, 125　Central line to ST. PAUL'S

Aldgate, 16, 17, 25　Circle or Metropolitan line to ALDGATE

Aldgate Pump, 19, 25　Circle or Metropolitan line to ALDGATE

All Hallows Barking-by-the-Tower, 10, 11, 15　Circle or District line to TOWER HILL

All Hallows, Lombard Street (Grass Church), 51, 55　Central or Northern line to BANK

All Hallows, London Wall, 36, 41　Central, Circle or Metropolitan line to LIVERPOOL STREET

All Hallows, Staining, 52, 53, 55　Circle or Metropolitan line to ALDGATE; Circle or District line to TOWER HILL

Austin Friars Church (Dutch Church), 37, 38, 41　Central or Northern line to BANK

Bacon, Nicholas, tomb, 135　See St. Paul's Cathedral

Baynard's Castle, Castle Baynard Pub, 148, 151　Circle or District line to BLACKFRIARS

Becket, Thomas, relic at Museum of London, 63　See London Bridge

Bevis Marks, xii, 25　Circle or Metropolitan line to ALDGATE

Billingsgate Market, 56, 57, 61　Circle or District line to MONUMENT

Bishop of Winchester's Palace, Rose Window, 179, 187　Northern line to LONDON BRIDGE or Circle or District line to MONUMENT and take a pleasant walk across London Bridge

Bishopsgate, 35　Central, Circle or Metropolitan line to LIVERPOOL STREET

Blackfriars, Dominican Priory of, 138, 139　Circle or District line to BLACKFRIARS (between Blackfriars Lane and St. Andrew's Hill)

Bowes, Martin, tomb, 54　See St. Mary Woolnoth

Brewers' Hall, 114, 117　Circle, Northern or Metropolitan line to MOORGATE

Carpenters' Hall, 36, 41　Central, Circle or Metropolitan line to LIVERPOOL STREET

Chapone, Peter, tomb, 13　See St. Olave, Hart Street

Charing Cross (Eleanor's Cross), 213, 222　Bakerloo, Jubilee or Northern line to CHARING CROSS

Charles I statue, site of Eleanor's Cross, 213, 222　Bakerloo, Jubilee or Northern line to CHARING CROSS

Charterhouse, 192–195, 204　Circle or Metropolitan line to BARBICAN

Christ Church, Greyfriars Monastery, 128, 129, 139　Central line to ST. PAUL'S

Civic Virtues at the Museum of London, 96, 97　See Guildhall and Museum of London

Cleary Garden, 143, 145　Circle or District line to MANSION HOUSE

Clifford's Inn, 169, 176　Circle or District line to TEMPLE

Clink, The, 179, 187　Northern line to LONDON BRIDGE

Cloth Fair House, ix, 177　Circle or Metropolitan line to BARBICAN

Cock Lane, 152　See Golden Boy

Coopers' Hall, 108, 109　Central or Northern line to BANK

Cordwainers' Hall, 140, 141　Central line to ST. PAUL'S

Cripplegate, 117　Circle, Metropolitan, or Northern line to MOORGATE

Crosby Hall, Site of, xiii, 35　Central or Northern line to BANK; the building, Crosby's house, has been moved to Chelsea, on Cheyne Walk between Old Church and Beaufort Streets. Nearest underground is Circle, District or Piccadilly line to SOUTH KENSINGTON. Walk towards the Thames. A suggested route: walk south along Onslow Square over to Fulham Road, west to Old Church Street, then south to Cheyne Walk and west to Danvers Street.

Drapers' Hall, 39, 41　Central or Northern line to BANK

Dutch Church, 37, 38　See Austin Friars Church

Eleanor's Coat of Arms (in the Museum of London), 127　See Great Cross at Cheap

Elsing Spital Tower, 111, 117　Circle, Metropolitan or Northern line to MOORGATE

Finsbury Fields (Finsbury Square), 190, 191, 203　Circle, Metropolitan or Northern line to MOORGATE

Fishmongers' Hall, 67–69　Circle or District line to MONUMENT

Frances, Countess of Sussex, tomb, 216　See Westminster Abbey

George, The, 51, 55　Central or Northern line to BANK

George Inn, Southwark, 184, 187   Northern line to LONDON BRIDGE

Girdlers' Hall, 106, 107, 109   Circle, Metropolitan or Northern line to MOORGATE

Golden Boy at Pie Corner, 152, 177   Central line to ST. PAUL'S

Great Cross at Cheap (Eleanor's Cross), 126, 127, 139   Central line to ST. PAUL'S

Gresham's Golden Grasshopper, 44
See Royal Exchange

Greyfriars Monastery, 128, 129
See Christ Church

Guildhall, 94–99, 101   Central or Northern line to BANK

Guy's Hospital (London Bridge arch), 63, 187   Northern line to LONDON BRIDGE

House at Cloth Fair, ix, 177   Circle or Metropolitan line to BARBICAN

Houses at Huggen Hill, 143
See Cleary Garden

Inner Temple, 172–176   Circle or District line to TEMPLE

Jewel Tower, 217
See Westminster, Palace of

King Sebert's Tomb, 216
See Westminster Abbey

King's Wardrobe, 149, 151   Circle or District line to BLACKFRIARS

Lambeth Palace, 220, 221, 223   Circle or District line to WESTMINSTER and walk south through Victoria Gardens to Lambeth Bridge. The palace is on the Southwark side of the Thames

Leadenhall Market, 26–29   Central or Northern line to BANK

Lincoln's Inn, 198–200, 205   Central or Piccadilly line to HOLBORN or Central line to CHANCERY LANE

Little Britain (houses), 118, 125   Central line to ST. PAUL'S

London Bridge, 62, 63, 69   Northern line to LONDON BRIDGE

London Bridge, arched alcove, 62, 63
See Guy's Hospital

London Bridge, stone bracket, 63
See Museum of London

London Stone, 74, 75, 79   Circle or District line to CANNON STREET

London Wall at Coopers Row, 22, 23, 25   Circle or District line to TOWER HILL

Ludgate, 139   Central line to ST. PAUL'S

Mansion House, 76, 79   Central or Northern line to BANK

Merchant Taylors' Hall, 40, 41   Central or Northern line to BANK

Monument, The, 66, 69   Circle or District line to MONUMENT

Moorgate, 203   Circle, Metropolitan or Northern line to MOORGATE

Museum of London, Central line to ST. PAUL'S and walk north along St. Martin's Le Grand
Becket, St. Thomas, relic of, 63
Eleanor's Coat of Arms, 127
Four Civic Virtues, The, 96, 97
Synagogue, 6, 7

Newgate, 177   Central line to ST. PAUL'S and walk west along Newgate Street

Old Bailey, 162, 163, 177   Central line to ST. PAUL'S

Painter Stainers' Hall, 143
See Cleary Garden

Pardon Churchyard, 194, 195
See Charterhouse

Paul's Cross, 134, 139   Central line to ST. PAUL'S

Pie Corner, 152, 177
See Golden Boy

Queen Elizabeth's Statue, 167
See St. Dunstan-in-the-West

Royal Exchange, 42, 44, 49   Central or Northern line to BANK

St. Alban's Tower, 112, 117   Central line to ST. PAUL'S

St. Alphage Churchyard, 113, 117   Circle, Metropolitan or Northern line to MOORGATE

St. Andrew, Holborn, 166, 176   Central line to CHANCERY LANE

St. Andrew Undershaft, xi, 20, 21, 25   Circle or Metropolitan line to ALDGATE

St. Andrew-by-the-Wardrobe, 148, 151   Circle or District line to BLACKFRIARS

St. Anne and St. Agnes, 121, 125   Central line to ST. PAUL'S

St. Augustine Papey, xii, 29   Central or Northern line to BANK and walk east along Cornhill and Leadenhall and down St. Mary Axe

St. Augustine-with-St. Faith (St. Augustine, Watling Street), 133, 139, 140   Central line to ST. PAUL'S

St. Bartholomew-the-Great, 156–159, 177   Circle or Metropolitan line to BARBICAN

St. Bartholomew-the-Less, 154, 155, 177　Circle or Metropolitan line to BARBICAN

St. Bartholomew's Medical College, 194　Circle or Metropolitan line to BARBICAN

St. Benet Fink, 41, 42　Central or Northern line to BANK

St. Benet, Paul's Wharf, 146, 147, 151　Circle or District line to BLACKFRIARS or Central line to ST. PAUL'S

St. Benet Sherehog, 92, 101　Central line to ST. PAUL'S and walk along New Change to Watling Street, down Watling Street to Queen Street, turn left onto Queen Street and Pancras Lane is on the right.

St. Botolph, Aldersgate, 122–125　Central line to ST. PAUL'S

St. Botolph, Aldgate, 4, 5, 7　Circle or Metropolitan line to ALDGATE

St. Botolph, Billingsgate, 61, 65　Circle or District line to MONUMENT

St. Botolph, Bishopsgate, 30, 31, 35　Central, Circle or Metropolitan line to LIVERPOOL STREET

St. Brides, 170, 171, 176　Circle or District line to BLACKFRIARS

St. Clare, Abbey of, 6, 7　Circle or Metropolitan line to ALDGATE

St. Clement Danes, 209–211　Circle or District line to TEMPLE

St. Clement, Eastcheap, 70, 73　Circle or District line to MONUMENT

St. Dunstan-in-the-East, 14, 15　Circle or District line to TOWER HILL

St. Dunstan-in-the-West, 167, 176　Circle or District line to TEMPLE

St. Edmund, King and Martyr, 51, 55　Central or Northern line to BANK

St. Ethelburga, 32, 33, 35　Central, Circle or Metropolitan line to LIVERPOOL STREET

St. Etheldreda, 164, 165, 176　Central line to CHANCERY LANE

St. Gabriel Fenchurch, 50, 55　Circle or Metropolitan line to ALDGATE and walk west along Aldgate and Fenchurch Street

St. Giles, Cripplegate, 115–117　Circle, Metropolitan, or Northern line to MOORGATE

St. Giles-in-the-Fields, 201, 205　Central or Northern line to TOTTENHAM COURT ROAD

St. Helen, Bishopsgate, 34, 35　Central, Circle or Metropolitan line to LIVERPOOL STREET and walk south along Bishopsgate

St. James, Garlickhythe, 86, 87　Circle or District line to MANSION HOUSE or CANNON STREET

St. James Palace, 214, 215, 222　Jubilee, Piccadilly or Victoria line to GREEN PARK

St. John the Baptist-upon-Walbrook, 78, 79　Circle or District line to CANNON STREET

St. John's Churchyard, 197, 204　Circle or Metropolitan line to BARBICAN or FARRINGDON

St. John's Gate, 196, 204　Circle or Metropolitan line to BARBICAN or FARRINGDON

St. John Zachary, 121, 125　Central line to ST. PAUL'S

St. Katherine Coleman, 24, 25　Circle or Metropolitan line to ALDGATE

St. Katherine Cree, 18, 25　Circle or Metropolitan line to ALDGATE

St. Katherine's Docks, 3, 7　Circle or District line to TOWER HILL

St. Katherine-by-the-Tower (St. Katherine's Hospital), 3, 7　Circle or District line to TOWER HILL

St. Lawrence Jewry, 99–101　Central or Northern line to BANK

St. Lawrence Pountney, 71, 73　Circle or District line to CANNON STREET

St. Leonard, Shoreditch, 188, 189, 203　Northern line to OLD STREET and walk east along Old Street to junction of Shoreditch High Street and Kingsland Road

St. Magnus the Martyr, 64, 65, 69　Circle or District line to MONUMENT

St. Margaret, Fish Street Hill, 66, 69　Circle or District line to MONUMENT

St. Margaret Lothbury, 104, 105　Central or Northern line to BANK

St. Margaret Pattens, 60, 61　Circle or District line to MONUMENT

St. Margaret, Westminster, 218, 223　Circle or District line to WESTMINSTER

St. Martin-in-the-Fields, 212, 222　Bakerloo, Jubilee or Northern line to CHARING CROSS

St. Martin-within-Ludgate, 136, 137, 139　Central line to ST. PAUL'S

St. Mary Abchurch, 72, 73　Circle or District to CANNON STREET

St. Mary Aldermanbury, 110, 117　Central or Northern line to BANK or Central line to ST. PAUL'S

St. Mary Aldermary, 88, 91　Circle or District line to MANSION HOUSE

St. Mary Axe, xii, 29　Central or Northern line to BANK and walk west along Cornhill and Leadenhall Street to and along St. Mary Axe

St. Mary of Bethleham, Hospital of, xii, 35　Central, Circle or Metropolitan line to LIVERPOOL STREET

St. Mary-le-Bow, 89, 91　Central line to ST. PAUL'S and walk east along Cheapside

St. Mary-at-Hill, 58, 59, 61　Circle or District line to TOWER HILL

St. Mary Overie's Dock, 178, 179, 187   Northern line to LONDON BRIDGE or Circle or District line to MONUMENT and walk across the bridge

St. Mary Somerset, 144, 145   Circle or District line to MANSION HOUSE

St. Mary Spital Hospital and Priory, xi, 203   Central, Circle or Metropolitan line to LIVERPOOL STREET

St. Mary Staining, 119, 125   Central line to ST. PAUL'S

St. Mary-le-Strand, 207, 211   Circle or District line to TEMPLE

St. Mary Woolchurch, 76, 79   See Mansion House

St. Mary Woolnoth, 54, 55   Central or Northern line to BANK

St. Michael at Bassishaw, 108, 109   Central or Northern line to BANK

St. Michael, Cornhill, 48, 49   Central or Northern line to BANK

St. Michael, Paternoster Royal, 84, 85, 87   Circle or District line to CANNON STREET

St. Mildred, Poultry, 77, 101   Central or Northern line to BANK

St. Nicholas, Cole Abbey, 142, 145   Central line to ST. PAUL'S

St. Olave, Hart Street, 12, 13, 15   Circle or District line to TOWER HILL

St. Olave, Jewry, 102, 103, 105   Central or Northern line to BANK

St. Olave, Silver Street, 120, 125, 225   Central line to ST. PAUL'S

St. Pancras, 92, 93, 101   Central or Northern line to BANK and walk along New Change to Watling Street, along Watling Street to Queen Street, turn left and Pancras Lane is on the right

St. Paul's Cathedral, 118, 130–135, 139   Central line to ST. PAUL'S

St. Peter, Cornhill, 46, 47, 49   Central or Northern line to BANK

St. Peter, Westcheap, 126, 127, 139   Central line to ST. PAUL'S

St. Sepulchre-without-Newgate, 160, 161, 177   Central line to ST. PAUL'S and walk west along Newgate Street

St. Stephen, Walbrook, 77, 79   Central or Northern line to BANK

St. Swithin, London Stone, 74, 75, 79   Circle or District line to CANNON STREET

St. Thomas's Hospital, 185–187   Northern line to LONDON BRIDGE

St. Vedast, Foster Lane, 134, 139   Central line to ST. PAUL'S

Salters' Hall, 113   Circle, Metropolitan, or Northern line to MOORGATE

Salters' Hall, original site, 141, Central line to ST. PAUL'S

Saracen's Head Inn, 163, 177   Central line to ST. PAUL'S

Savoy Chapel, 208, 211   Bakerloo, Jubilee, or Northern line to CHARING CROSS and walk northeast along the Strand to Savoy Street; or Bakerloo, Circle, District, or Northern line to EMBANKMENT and walk northeast along the Embankment to Savoy Street

Scaffold at Tower Hill, 8, 9, 15   Circle or District line to TOWER HILL

Skinners' Hall, 80, 81, 83   Circle or District line to CANNON STREET

Smithfield Market, 153, 177   Circle or Metropolitan line to BARBICAN

Somerset House, 206, 211   Circle or District line to TEMPLE

Southwark Cathedral (St. Mary Overie), 180–183, 187   Northern line to LONDON BRIDGE or Circle or District line to MONUMENT and walk across bridge

Spital Cross, xi, 129   See St. Mary Spital Hospital

Standard at Cornhill, 43, 49   Central or Northern line to BANK

Staple Inn, Holborn, 168, 176   Central line to CHANCERY LANE

Stationers' Hall, 150, 151   Central line to ST. PAUL'S

Stocks Market, 76, 79   See Mansion House

Stone Bracket from London Bridge, 63   See London Bridge

Stow, John, tomb, xi   See St. Andrew Undershaft

Synagogue, 6   See Abbey of St. Clare and Museum of London

Tallow Chandlers' Hall, 82, 83   Circle or District line to CANNON STREET

Temple Church, 174   See Inner Temple

Throckmorton, Nicholas, tomb, 18   See St. Katherine Cree

Tower of London, facing page 1, 1, 2, 7   Circle or District line to TOWER HILL

Tun at Cornhill, 45, 49   Central or Northern line to BANK

Tyburn, 202, 205   Central line to MARBLE ARCH

Westminster Abbey (Monastery of Westminster), 216, 223   Circle or District line to WESTMINSTER

Westminster Hall, 219   See Westminster, Palace of

Westminster, Palace of, 217, 219, 223   Circle or
    District line to WESTMINSTER
White Tower, 1
    See Tower of London
Whittington, Dick Cat on Highgate Hill, x
    Northern line to ARCHWAY
Windmill Pub, 191
    See Finsbury Fields

A List of Maps

Portesoken Warde 7
Tower Streete Warde 15
Aldgate Warde 25
Limestreete Warde 29
Bishopsgate Warde 35
Brodestreete Warde 41
Cornehill Warde 49
Langborne Warde 55
Billinsgate Warde 61
Bridge Warde Within 69
Candlewicke Street Warde 73
Walbrooke Warde 79
Downegate Warde 83
Vintry Warde 87
Cordwainer Street Ward 91
Cheape Warde 101
Coleman Street Warde 105
Bassings Hall Warde 109
Creplesgate Warde 117
Aldersgate Warde 125
Faringdon Ward Within 139
Bredstreete Warde 141
Queene Hithe Warde 145
Castle Baynard Warde 151
Faringdon Warde Without 176–177
Borough of Southwarke and Bridge Warde
    Without 187
The Suburbes Without the Walles 203–205
Liberties of the Dutchie of Lancaster 211
The Citie of Westminster 222–223

COLOPHON

This book was written, illustrated, and designed by Arline K. Thomson, composed in ITC New Baskerville in QuarkXpress, and printed on 60# basis Mohawk Vellum Offset by the University of Maine Printing Services.

The paper edition was bound by the University of Maine Printing Services.

The cloth edition was bound by New Hampshire Bindery.